THE NEW

According to the Perar

NORTH
WEST · EAST
SOUTH

Forest Boundary .—.—.
Roads dividing the
Northern, Middle &
Southern Areas ══
Railways. ──
Heathland. ░░░░
Cultivation. ☐
Only the main roads
are shewn . H.S.

To Sthton.
Brockis hill.
Bucketts.
Ironshill.
Lynd—hurst road.
Ashurst.
Deer leap.
y—d—hurst
Matley.
Beaulieu rive
Park Hill.
Denny.
Beaulieu Road.
Iptey.
Ramnor.
Bishop's Ditch.
Culverley.
Hertford Heath.
New park
Pignal.
Woodfidley.
Buttsash.
Balmer Lawn.
Holbury.
Frame wood.
Hilltop.
Beau—Lieu.
Broc zen urst
Wittley bridge.
Ladycross.
To Fawley.
Hatchet Pond.
Beufre.
Beaulieu Heath.
Bucklershard.
Setley.
Darkwater
Ex bury depe.
Boldre.
St Leonards.
Needsore
Vicarshill.
Bergerie.
Sowley Pond.
Buckland Rings.
The Solent.
Lymington.

0.   12.   14.   16.   18.   20

5/31 £2.99

THE
NEW FOREST

HEYWOOD SUMNER

THE
NEW FOREST

THE DOLPHIN PRESS
CHRISTCHURCH

Published in Great Britain by
THE DOLPHIN PRESS
176 Barrack Road, Christchurch, Hants.

ISBN O 85642 006 4

1st Edition, February 1924
2nd Edition, April 1925
3rd Revised and Enlarged Edition, September 1972

Printed in Great Britain
by the Rochdale Times Ltd.,
Rochdale, Lancs.

Bound by James Burn at
Esher, Surrey

CONTENTS

ILLUSTRATIONS

B

Introduction

★

THE ARCHAEOLOGY
by
MICHAEL RIDLEY, F.S.A. SCOT. F.R.A.I.

THE New Forest is situated in one of the richest archaeological areas in the country. Over the years it has
changed, and the men of various periods of history saw
it differently. As an area for archaeological research it
has for long been neglected, archaeologists tending to
concentrate on the more easily accessible remains which
surround it. In recent years this has changed and much
valuable information is being obtained from within the
wooded areas and the heathland.

Heywood Sumner was a pioneer in the field of observation, he knew the Forest intimately and noted every
detail in every season. He was also one of the first to
observe the archaeological remains and practise what
we know today as Field Archaeology. In addition to his
field observation he carried out a number of excavations
on Roman pottery kilns and on what he termed 'pre-
Roman earthworks.' These activities resulted in the
publication of his 'Ancient Earthworks of the New
Forest' and his work on New Forest Pottery as well as
a number of minor publications. In this present book

he lays before the reader a mine of information on all aspects of the Forest, collected and researched first hand and from personal observation. This third edition has been revised and enlarged to include his descriptions of the areas immediately adjacent to the Forest boundary.

The majority of Heywood Sumner's archaeological observations remain as valid today as when he first wrote them although there are one or two exceptions. These are mainly confined to his datings of certain features. The earliest artifacts of man which occur in the Forest are flint hand axes of the Palaeolithic period, the Old Stone Age. These are found in gravel pits which line the forest side of the Avon Valley from Alderbury to Rockford. A number of Palaeolithic axes were found during the early part of this century, the period when Heywood Sumner was active. Specimens then could be purchased for a few shillings from the gravel workers. Today the story is different, the gravel is dug mechanically by such methods which do not allow the discovery of specimens. Although I have observed the pits at Rockford Common over a number of years, I have not seen one Palaeolithic axe discovered. Palaeolithic implements have been found at Wood Green, Fordingbridge, and along the coast from Chewton Bunny to Milford.

In September 1930, the remains of a large fragment of mammoth tusk was found in the Avon Valley drift gravel at Ibsley near Rockford. The discovery was due to the astute observation of the driver of a steam crane who noticed the bone lying on the newly scraped gravel surface. Several attempts were made to remove the fragment, which measured 3′ 10″ in length but they were unsuccessful and the bone disintegrated.

In his original 'prehistoric' introduction to the book, Heywood Sumner omits mention of the Mesolithic period. Today we are aware that areas of the Forest were inhabited by Mesolithic man and it is possible occasionally to find implements of the period testifying to his presence. The evidence is such, however, to suggest that the Mesolithic population was by no means large. Mesolithic man lived in an afforested environment, but he may have made some attempt at deforestation. This was about 8,000 years ago.

Efforts in deforestation became more pronounced during the succeeding Neolithic period, the new Stone Age. The Neolithic period is sometimes known as the Neolithic revolution. It was a gradual revolution during which man changed his social economy from food gathering to food producing. His agricultural methods were, however, crude and it was not until more sophisticated methods came into use during the Bronze Age that efforts in woodland clearance had much success. Evidence of Neolithic man in the Forest is scarce, however isolated finds of flint implements have been found in a number of places, but no evidence of Neolithic settlement has been found. This does not mean that Neolithic man did not live in the Forest, simply that modern archaeologists have not found evidence. Neolithic implements have been found at Eyeworth and Furzehill, below Picked Post. A polished flint axe was found at Gorley Hill and in 1969 a fine polished axe was found during the excavations of a Bronze Age site on Rockford Common.

The Bronze Age is probably the best represented of all periods in the Forest. Visible remains of the work of Bronze Age men occur in abundance. The most prolific are the earthen barrows, the sepulchral mounds. These are dotted all over the Forest. Barrows can be found on Beaulieu Heath, Sway Common, Setley Plain, and near Thorny Hill, Denny and Matley. A number are scattered over the gravel hills of the Northern area. The Archaeological Division of the Ordnance Survey has recorded 176 round barrows in the Forest. This gives only a rough indication as a number have been destroyed or mutilated. While excavating a Bronze Age crema- tion cemetery on Rockford Common recently, I discovered the ploughed out remains of two round barrows. Neither the barrows nor the cremation cemetery was visible on the original ground surface due to ploughing during the 18th century and it was only due to stripping prior to gravel extraction that the features became visible. Remains of occupation by the Secondary Neolithic Beaker People was also found on the site. A similar cremation cemetery was found and excavated by Heywood Sumner at Ibsley Common. In addition to the flint implements of the period, bronze tools have also been found and recently a bronze axe was unearthed at a gravel pit at Ibsley.

Recent analysis of the pollen preserved in the old soil surfaces under barrows which have been excavated have given us some idea of land use during the period. Examination of the pollen beneath a late Bronze Age barrow at Berry Wood suggested that the barrow was constructed on or near agricultural land which may have been abandoned.

Not all the barrows are of Bronze Age date. One on Hatchet Moor excavated 1941-42 proved to be of the Iron Age and of a unique character. The remains of what appeared to be an Iron Age cart burial being unearthed. The Iron Age is principally represented by Hill forts and enclosures. Buckland Rings and Ampress were placed at a vantage point on the upper estuary of the Lymington River, while the fort at Exbury con- trolled the estuary of the Beaulieu River. Other forts were situated at Godmanescap, Goshill Wood, Roe Wood, Castle Hill, Burley, and Malwood Castle.

Heywood Sumner refers to most of these as 'pre- Roman,' but includes them in his Bronze Age descrip- tion. The area was important during the Iron Age.

Hengistbury Head, formerly within the New Forest Boundary, is one of the foremost Iron Age settlement sites in Southern Britain. Its promontory fort encloses a large area which when partially excavated by Bushe-Fox in 1911-12 produced large numbers of coins minted on the site as well as huge quantities of pottery and other artifacts.

Little is known about the part the area played during the early days of the Roman invasion. Sufficient remains, however, to indicate that it was important strategically as it lay directly in the path of the Roman advance towards Dorset.

The people of Hengistbury belonged to the Durotrigian trible, and Hengistbury seems to have been an important town, if not an area capital. The interesting fact to note is that, unlike Maiden Castle, near Dorchester, which has yielded ample evidence of Roman attack, Hengistbury has not. All the evidence points to a long and continuous association with the Romans before, during and after their invasion. This is unusual, but a parallel can be found in the Chichester area, ruled by the great Romano-Briton, Cogidubnus. Excavations on Hengistbury revealed no burnt huts, no hurried burials, but a continuous sequence of Roman pottery, dating from the first century B.C. to the New Forest pottery of the Romano-British period. Hengistbury coins were minted after the Roman invasion and were found alongside Roman coins. The people, then, seem to have been little troubled by the Romans, who allowed them to retain their own way of life. They were tolerant of, even friendly with Rome, trading with them, the Romans on their part, by-passing them on condition that they remained friendly. Recent discoveries of a Roman fort on St. Catherine's Hill, which overlooks Hengistbury Head and the river ways into Wessex, indicate that the Romans, however, thought it advisable

11

to retain a small garrison in the area to keep an eye on them.

Later evidence of Roman occupation is provided by the numerous sites of pottery kilns which are found in the Forest. During the 3rd and 4th century A.D. these kilns produced vast quantities of what is known as 'New Forest' ware which was traded and used throughout Britain.

The fabric is hard and the shapes attractive and wheel turned. Decoration is often slip applied or incised. A number of these kilns were excavated by Heywood Sumner. Recently further excavations have been carried out by Mrs. Valerie Swann and Miss E. M. Collinson. Kilns have been found in the Northern area of the Forest, the valley of Dockens Water, Latchmore Brook and in Ashley Hole. Well-known sites are the kilns at Sloden and Crock Hill. To-date no indication of the presence of a Roman villa has come to light.

Heywood Sumner was a pioneer observer of the antiquities of the Forest. Although we can now add to his account of the prehistory, his account of the topography of the Forest, though not of great length or detail, remains as vital and fresh as the day it was written and will continue to be one of the most readable accounts of the Forest. His story starts with the historical period.

CHAPTER ONE

★

Historical Background

THE Anglo-Saxon Chronicle gives brief entries that tell of traditional fighting in this District between the Britons and the invading West Saxons from 495 to 519 A.D. and onwards. The latter date marks the battle of Charford, or Cerdicsford, near Downton, and the establishment of the West Saxon domination thus far. The Moot earthwork at Downton, just outside our Northern limit, is a very fine example of a Saxon open-air court of Justice. The numerous place-names ending in *ton* (homestead), round Lymington indicate Saxon or Jutish occupation, and the seafarers' camp at Ampress may belong to this period, a supposition supported by the adjacent Norse names of *Rossen* and *Askin* Guters ; while the "herepaths" (warpaths), named in the Saxon boundaries of Ringwood and Downton, tell us that these ways were used in Saxon times.

Our Danish evidence is only inference. Thus : William I justified his tyrannical Forest laws by producing a document which purported to be a Charter of Canute the Dane in which the exclusive right of chase was vested in the King. The forgery, and the acceptance of this document suggest that it must have been supported by the tradition of Canute having used the Forest for the pleasure of the Chase.

William I made the New Forest in 1079 A.D. as recorded in the Saxon Chronicle by one "who had known him, who had looked upon him, and who had once lived at his court. . . . He made large Forests for the deer and enacted laws therewith, so whoever killed a hart or a hind should be blinded. As he forbade killing the deer, so also the boars, and he loved the tall stags as if he was their father. He also appointed concerning the hares that they should go free. The rich complained and the poor murmured, but he was so sturdy that he recked nought of them; they must will all that the King willed if they would live; or would keep their lands; or would hold their possessions; or would be maintained in their rights —alas! that any man should so exalt himself, and carry himself in this pride over all!"

This Anglo-Saxon Chronicler had no bias in favour of William I. Surely he would have recorded the destruction of many churches and villages, as later monkish chroniclers asserted—if such destruction had been dealt when "large Forests" were thus made? There is no evidence that this District has ever been under cultivation, or thickly populated, and the prevailing poverty of its soil bears witness to the reason. Barbarous Forest laws, together with a certain amount of eviction, were sufficient causes for complaint and murmurs from rich and poor. William Rufus made bad, worse, when he enacted the death penalty for offences against his Forest laws. This brutal injustice was repealed by Henry III, but until the reign of James I the Forest laws retained their original character of feudal oppression, in theory, if not in practice. Since then, Forest legislation has been principally concerned with the use and abuse of woodlands. The Deer Removal Act of 1851, and the New Forest Act of 1877, finally changed the purpose for which William I made the New Forest eight hundred and forty-five years ago, i.e., for the preservation of the King's deer. Recent legislation has tended to regard it as "an open space for recreation and enjoyment," subject to rights belonging to the Crown and to the Commoners.

CHAPTER TWO

★

The Present

If the reader looks at the map of the New Forest he will see that it is divided into three areas by roads leading from Ringwood, to Cadnam, on to Romsey ; and from Lymington, to Lyndhurst, on to Southampton. Divided thus :

THE NORTHERN AREA includes the highest heathlands of the Forest.

THE MIDDLE AREA is for the most part over-grown by great woods.

THE SOUTHERN AREA is wooded lowland, and gradually becomes the seaboard of the Solent.

The characteristics of these three areas are distinct, and the topography of the District will be understood better if they are explored in turn, than if the wayfarer wanders at large within the Forest Boundary limit. Accordingly, the plan of this Guide is to give a separate description of each of the areas named, followed by notes referring to woodlands, places of interest, etc., arranged in alphabetical order. These notes aim at supplying

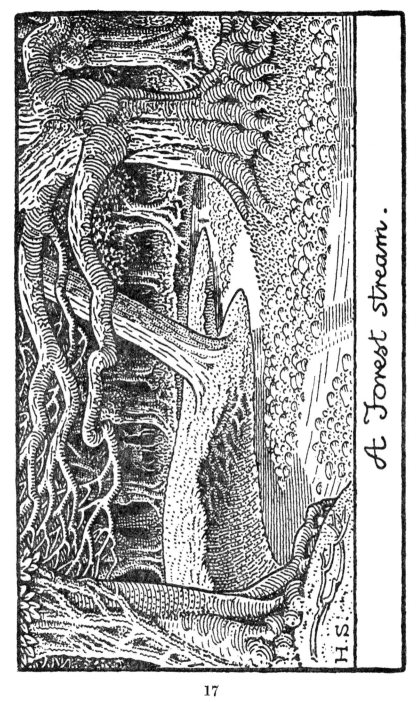

A Forest Stream.

H.S.

17

compass direction rather than *signpost* direction, for the finding of ways by map and landmark is one of the stray pleasures that fulfil a day spent in the Forest, and the hidden beauties thus revealed belong to the finders as their own discoveries and possessions.

The map on the inside cover aims at supplying general knowledge of the District. It only deals with the distribution of woodland, heathland and cultivation, the streams, the principal place-names, and the main roads.

The water-parting ridge of the Forest District should be noted, rising from Buckland Rings, on to Wilverley, Castle Hill Burley, Bratley, Ocknell to Fritham and Bramshaw Telegraph. This line was probably the prehistoric way inland. On one side of this ridge the streams flow down to the Avon on the other, to the Test, Southampton Water and the Solent.

★

The Northern Area

Headquarters : *Ringwood, Fordingbridge, Brook, Stonycross.*

Landmarks : *Picked Post, Ocknell clump, Amberwood, Sloden Hill, Bramshaw Telegraph, Bramble Hill.*

THE main feature of the Northern area is open moorland—level, upland plains, capped with gravel, covered with heather, furze and bracken, worn into five parallel ridges and bottoms by streams that trickle in dry, and rush in wet weather down to the Avon. Here and there the hills are overgrown with thickets, with old woods, with planted enclosures, or with self-sown Scots pine, but the open Forest is never far distant. From all the roads and tracks the wayfarer sees far views over wild foregrounds to distant cultivation, over a tract of primaeval waste set in the midst of a more fertile formation, over heathlands surrounded by the chalk hills of Dorset, Wiltshire, Hampshire and the Isle of Wight. The lie of the land and the vegetation show that the sandy, gravelly, clayey soil of the Forest rests on a chalk basin that extends from Cranborne Chase to "the Island," and from Purbeck to Hampshire South Downs.

The streams in this area run down parallel bottoms,

as before said, separated by gravel-topped ridges terminating in bluffs which line the Forest side of the Avon valley. Each of these bottoms has its own special character, follow a stream, or follow a ridge, are the best directions for those who seek to find wild beauty for themselves. In following these streams and ridges the outflow of hill-side springs should be noticed. The sheets of plateau gravel that cap these hill-tops are only of a few feet in thickness, and they rest on sand, below which is clay. The surface water, percolating through the super-imposed gravel and sand, is held up by the clay, and peezes out of the hill-sides through the exit of least resistance : then behold, a spring ! "Jack and Jill went up a hill, to fetch a pail of water." So do we, here, and the water does not fail. But in times of summer drought, the overflow of such hill-side springs is absorbed by the thirsty soil long before it reaches the brook below. Thus the dry brook is not evidence of the waterless state of this district. Drought has robbed the supply by the way. Even in 1911 and 1921 our hill-side springs did not fail : but their outflow appears to be partially governed by aerial pressure, i.e., held up by the air conditions that create a rising barometer. These springs will rise when the barometer falls, at the end of a dry spell, before the rain falls.

Within this century blackcocks curled on these hills, now alas, they have died out, but the desolate cry of curlews may still be heard in the spring. Forest bird lore is rightly kept secret, by those that observe and know ; no secret, however, is told when I say that bird lovers will find plenty to observe, throughout the Forest.

Deer are supposed not to exist in the Forest, according to the Deer Removal Act of 1851 ; but fortunately a remnant still survives. When this Act was passed the fallow deer numbered from three thousand to four thousand. Now they may be counted in fifties instead of thousands. They are absolutely wild and uncared for. The keepers no longer cut "browse"—holly-tops, ivy, etc.,—for their winter feed, though "browse-pen" field-names still survive. Notwithstanding, they thrive, and would multiply if they were not shot. The New Forest Deer-hounds take an annual toll, but this has been insufficient to keep down their numbers, and in late years they have been greatly reduced by buck-shot. The red deer may be indigenous. Their number has been decreasing, and now, does not probably exceed twelve. The fallow deer are said to be the descendants of an Asiatic breed introduced by the Romans, and probably number from one hundred and fifty to two hundred. Ten years ago they were more numerous. I have counted a head of twenty-nine in Greenford Bottom, and G. H. Slightam, who was keeper at Ashley Lodge, has counted a herd of forty-six in his Walk; whereas now, one rarely sees five or six deer together, the result of decimation by shooting, not of natural, unfavourable conditions.

The New Forest fallow deer have this unusual characteristic, in summer their coats are golden buff with white spots, in winter they change to dun colour with light dun on the under side of their bodies. Fallow deer in parks have coats of either of these colours, but retain their respective colours both in summer and winter.

There is an interesting record quoted by the Hon. Gerald Lascelles in *Thirty-five Years in the New Forest*, stating the number of deer in the Forest in 1670 A.D. "*View of the Deere in the new fforest totall of ye Red Deere 357. Totall of ye ffallow Deere 7593.*" Of these, two hundred and fifty-four were entered as *Red Rascall*, and six thousand one hundred and eighty-four as *ffallow Rascall*. Rascall—*bestys of venery, or of chace or rascall*, was a Norman French term for deer not worth hunting, and the above numbers suggest that they included hinds and does. The hart till he was six years old was accounted *Rascayle* (Skeat). Shakespeare uses the term in *As You Like It*. Act III Scene III. *"Horns? . . . The noblest deer hath them as huge as the rascal."*

Roe deer, which abound in parts of Dorset, especially around Milton Abbas, are rarely seen on this side of the Avon. In Romano-British times Roe deer were far more numerous than red deer, judging by their respective bone relics found in excavations on Cranborne Chase by General Pitt-Rivers. It is unfortunate that bone perishes here, owing to acids that affect the percolating surface water in Tertiary soil, accordingly excavation in New Forest soil yields no bone evidence for comparison.

The deer, as before said, have been dispossessed of the Forest, in their stead ponies have entered into possession. A stranger may supose that the ponies are wild, seeing that they wander at will througout the Forest. They pay no heed to commoners' cattle-call "woaee, woaee," and they are deaf to the "kip, kip," call which summons work-a-day ponies near small holdings; in winter their rough coats stand up like door-mats as they nib, and twiddle, and bruise, and slowly chew the furze shoots; in summer they are almost sleek as they feed with their foals on the grassy lawns; but summer or winter they haunt plains and bogs and old woodlands without any apparent ownership. Yet it is not so. Every one belongs to somebody who knows where to find his ponies, while the agistors know them all, for it is one of their duties to see that the ponies in their District are tail-marked—the sign of the Forest fee having been paid. Although they range at will the same ponies more or less haunt a district, and rarely wander far beyond the feeding grounds which are theirs by right of occupancy.

"The Association for the Improvement of the Breed of Forest Ponies" holds an annual show in April at

Lyndhurst, and gives premiums and prizes for the best pony sires that are to run in the Forest; and the breed is further helped by "The Burley and District New Forest Pony and Cattle Society" which holds an annual show in August at Burley, and which aims at improving the breed of Forest mares.

Throughout the Forest there are special places where ponies and cattle congregate in summer—places where breezes always blow though hot air quivers above the heath, and where flies merely tease, but do not torment, as they do in the still woods. Such places are called "shades" in local speech—shade meaning a cool place. Generally shades are on high ground where ponds lie on the plains, for example, in this part of the Forest, Ocknell Pond, Janesmoor Pond, Longcross Pond, Stony Cross, Handy Cross Pond, Broomy Plain Pond, and Latchmore (the last being on open, but not high ground). On sunny, summer mornings, quite early, ponies, foals and cattle make dewy tracks from their feeding grounds to the shade that serves their haunt; there they will bide throughout the hot hours of a long summer's day, when flies are bold, shifting, whisking, stamping, nibbling unceasingly, making the best of a bad time, until the cool of the evening descends, and then they disperse to feed, unmolested by flies, amid lawns and thickets where nightjars churr in the gloaming.

Observant explorers on these heaths may notice small, embanked, rectangular areas which occur at Hive Garn Gutter, nearly Ashley Rails; on Isbley Common; in Newlands above Moyles Court; on Rockford Common; and at Pinnick above Greenford Bottom; and they may question their purpose. Such relics tell of a custom that was followed by local bee-keepers until about one hundred years ago. They used to send their hives to the Forest heathlands when the heather was in bloom, in order that their honey might profit thereby. Some neighbouring forester looked after them, and kept them in such embanked "bee-gardens" secure from disturbance by ponies or cattle. This custom is remembered as heresay by old men now living, but has quite died out.

Large commons adjoin the confines of this area, namely, on the West—Bisterne, Kingston, Rockford, Ibsley, Gorley and Hyde Commons, and on the North-East—Hamptworth, Landford, No Man's Land, Plaitford, Furzeley and Cadnam Commons, all of which are similar in character to the Forest heathlands, but their common rights are different, and of more value to the fortunate commoners.

PLACES OF INTEREST

AMBERWOOD. Planted in 1815. Oak with thorn and holly undergrowth, and an outer belt of Scots pine, cut in 1918. In the same year a clearing for a nursery was made within the wood South of Amberwood Cottage. Roman pottery and quern stones (for grinding corn) were found in grubbing up the tree roots, this site may have been occupied by the potters who worked at Crock Hill near by. There is a good track from here to Hyde, and rough tracks to Bramshaw Telegraph and to Fritham.

ANSES. Old beech, oak and holly. The regeneration of an old wood by self-sown seedlings may be well seen here, for the young trees are protected from the nibbling ponies and cattle by dense thickets of holly out of which they rise. This wood is remarkable for its great beeches —the largest of which is seventeen feet six inches in girth at four feet from the ground—and for its numerous examples of ingrowth—of branches growing into each other, or into the parent stem. The lower part of Anses is bounded by the twisting upper course of

Anses.

Dockenswater which perfects the charm of this, the most beautifully wooded bottom in the Northern area.

ASHLEY LODGE is a Crown keeper's cottage, built in 1773 near the site of an older lodge. Pitt's wood adjoins the grounds of Ashley Lodge, and its name commemorates John Pitt, surveyor general of the Forest when this wood was planted in 1775. It stands below the hills of Ticketsbury on the South and of Cockley Plain on the North, in a little valley down which meanders the Ashley brook to join Ditch-end brook near Green House Farm. In 1903 it was reinclosed, partly planted with Scots pine, larch and oak, and a nursery made at the Western end.

By kind permission of Mr. V. F. Leese, Deputy Surveyor of the New Forest, I have recently excavated a Roman pottery site at Ashley Rails, and amongst other things found eleven almost perfect vessels, which are now in the British Museum, besides numerous specimen sherds of "stamped ware"—a ware which had not previously been supposed to have been made in Britain. The coins found dated from Antoninus Pius (138-161 A.D.) to Constantine the Great (306-337 A.D.) *cf Roman Pottery made at Ashley Rails*, by the author.

There are good tracks from here to Hyde and to Godshill.

BENTLEY, NORTH AND SOUTH. Planted in 1700. Both are pure oak woods of fine growth.

BRAMBLE HILL. A beautiful, old wood, mostly beech. On the Southern slope of the hill is a large residence built on the site of a Forest Lodge. Pipers Weight (cf. Denny Wait, in the Southern area; *walt*, old English for water), North of Bramble Hill, is the highest ground in the District, four hundred and twenty-two feet above the sea.

BRAMSHAW CHURCH had the curious distinction of standing in Hampshire and Wiltshire, but in

1895 the Wiltshire portion of the parish was transferred to Hampshire. Bramshaw Wood is said to have provided the timber used in building Salisbury Cathedral (1220-1258).

BRAMSHAW TELEGRAPH is marked by a belt of Scots pines that crowns the ridge, four hundred and nineteen feet above the sea, whereon the highroads from Fordingbridge and Downton join on their way to Southampton. This was one of a chain of stations on high ground that was used during the first half of the nineteenth century for conveying messages by semaphore signals (Greek *sema*, a sign, and *ferein*, to bear), from Plymouth to London and vice versa. The Telegraph station was occupied by an officer and two men, one of whom was always on the look-out. The next stations going North-East were, Telegraph Wood, Toot Hill near Chilworth, Farley, the hill above Winchester Gaol, Telegraph Hill, Chessford Head, Four Marks, Monkwood Binstead (where I remember the derelict semaphore still standing in 1870). From here this line joined on to the line of Telegraph stations connecting Portsmouth with London. Going South-West, Telegraph Hill near Verwood, Chalbury Hill, Blandford race-down (on the South side of the long barrow), Bell Hill, Nettlecomb Tout, High Stoy, Toller Down (above Beaminster), Lambert's Castle, and so on to Plymouth. In Vol. XI of the Dorset Field Club transactions Mr. T. B. Groves gives a reproduction of a contemporaneous drawing of the old Telegraph station at High Stoy, Dorset, showing the original, shuttered type of "Murray" Telegraph (so called after the inventor, Lord George Murray). This type Mr. Groves states was superseded in 1816 by the semaphore mast with two arms, invented by Sir Home Popham, which type continued in use until 1847.

Mr. G. N. Godwin in *The Hampshire Antiquary*,

Vol. I, tells us that : "The use of semaphores was introduced into England from France in 1795. There were
ten between London and Portsmouth ; and one on
Southsea common was kept at work all day long. The
transmission of messages by them was described as
having been as quick as the transit of a discharged
cannon-ball. They sent Greenwich time daily to Portsmouth in about forty-five seconds. They were worked
in a very simple way, three or four persons being at
each station; and there were in all sixty-seven signals
representing letters, figures and phrases. The last mes-
sage along the London and Portsmouth line was sent in
1847."

When the electric telegraph was invented a question
was asked in Parliament as to the Government's atti-
tude towards the invention? To which the responsible
minister replied that the transmission of messages by
the Semaphore Telegraph was then so perfect that it
was not likely to be improved on, and certainly not by
adoption of the ingenious toy mentioned by the Hon.
Member !

The Semaphore Telegraph Tower of Montlhery on
the road to Orleans plays a part in *The Count of Monte-
Cristo* by Alexandre Dumas. Vol. II chaps. viii and ix,
and the incidental description gives particulars to such a
station in France. But in this instance, perhaps to suit
the needs of romance, the Telegraph was worked by
only one man.

BROOK is a typical hamlet on the edge of the Forest.
It belongs to Bramshaw parish, and is situated in a
spacious semi-circular valley-head below Stony Cross
and Fritham. The ill-omened name of Gibbet Wood,
below Salisbury trench, is said to record a gibbet
which stood there in the days when such dreadful display
was supposed to proclaim the reign of law and justice.
(cf, the tale of castaways on an unknown land, seeing

a gibbet, and saying : "*Thank God, we are in a civilised country.*")

BROOMY. Planted in 1809, mostly oak with bracken undergrowth. Broomy Lodge is a private residence. Holly Hatch, a woodman's cottage beside Dockenswater. The view Westward from Broomy Plain is very extensive. There are by-roads from here to Linwood, and to the Ringwood and Romsey high-road. Stagshorn moss and lilies-of-the-valley may be found near here by those who know where to look for them.

CADNAM is a hamlet lying partly in the parish of Ealing, and partly in that of Minstead. It was famous for an oak which, like the Glastonbury thorn, was reputed to come into leaf on old Christmas day (Jan. 6). Gilpin in his *Remarks on Forest Scenery*, describes the premature vegetation of this tree as follows : "Having often heard of this oak, I took a ride to see it on the 29th day of December, 1781. It was pointed out to me among several other oaks, surrounded by a little Forest stream, winding round a knoll, on which they stood. It is a tall, straight plant of no great age, and apparently vigorous ; except that its top has been injured ; from which several branches issue in the form of pollard shoots. It was entirely bare of leaves, as far as I could discern, when I saw it ; and undistinguishable from the other oaks in its neighbourhood ; except that its bark seemed rather smoother, occasioned I apprehended, only by frequent climbing. Having had the account of its early budding confirmed on the spot, I engaged one Michael Lawrence, who kept the White Hart, a small alehouse in the neighbourhood, to send me some of the leaves to Vicar's Hill, as soon as they should appear. The man, who had not the least doubt about the matter, kept his word ; and sent me several twigs on the morning of the 5th January, 1782 ; a few hours after they had been gathered. The leaves were fairly expanded ; and about an inch in length. From some of the buds two leaves had unsheathed themselves; but in general only one" . . . . "This early spring, however, of the Cadenham oak is of very short duration. The buds after unfolding themselves make no further progress; but immediately shrink from the season and die. The tree continues torpid, like other deciduous trees, during the remainder of the winter, and vegetates again in the spring, at the usual season." Two points may be noted in this account. (1) It mentions that the tree had been injured. (2) Twigs, with leaves on them, are assumed to represent similar vegetation all over the tree. A "super-annivated" Cadnam woodman tells me that the only evidence of such traditional growth is to be found in premature shoots around tree injuries, where young sap meets with old spine wood, and such premature budding is local, around the injury, not all over the tree. I give (and retain) this saying for future observation.

CANTERTON is in the parish of Minstead. At the junction of King's Garn Gutter and Coalmere brook, there are curious earthworks adjoining, that appear to mark the site of a mediaeval mill of which there is record (cf *Victoria History of Hampshire*).

CROCK HILL is between Amberwood and Islands Thorns, and is one of the New Forest Pottery sites where fine ware was produced in Roman times. This site has recently been replanted with silver fir beneath a canopy of oak planted in 1850.

EYEWORTH is an old beech wood with holly undergrowth. A specially fine tree that stands on the verge of Eyeworth and Studley is known as the "Queen beech"; its trunk rises about twenty feet from the ground without a fork, and measures sixteen feet ten inches in girth, four feet from the ground. In growth this tree compares with a fine beech beside the Lyndhurst Road in Burley Manor Park which measures

30

fourteen feet seven inches in girth, four feet from the ground. There was a powder factory on the Southern side of the wood.

"Avare," is the Domesday version of this place-name. It is interesting to note that locally, Eyeworth, of the Ordnance Survey, is still locally pronounced *Iver*, and used to be 150 years ago, cf "Ivory Lodge," a site here recorded in *Warner's Collections for a History of Hampshire. Ivers* as a place-suffix occurs along the Ebble and Nadder valleys; and marks what is called in Petersfield district, "a hanger," i.e., a wood on a steep hill. Perhaps connected with "oves", eaves, the edges of a declivity.

FORDINGBRIDGE is outside the Forest Boundary, but the following old custom connected with the Forest has been recorded : "The Lord of the Manor of Fordingbridge was obliged during the 'fence month' (i.e., fifteen days before and after Midsummer day), to keep watch, and ward upon the bridge spanning the Avon here, as by this way only could persons leave the Forest on the North-West side. The watch was summoned and set by the High Constable in these words : 'I, A. B. High Constable of the Hundred of Ford, so command you, and each of you, on behalf of our most gracious Sovereign Lord the King, to keep watch on this bridge until sunrise, and to detain all persons who shall be found to have in their possession venison taken from the New Forest, the property of His Majesty the King. Herein fail not at your peril.' The weapons then delivered to the guard resembled a pike, or hurdler's hook having an eight foot handle. On the approach of carts of suspected deer-stealers, the guards by lowering their pikes to a horizontal position, and holding one extremity against the body, while the hooked end rested on the iron railings of the bridge, presented a substantial barrier to the passage of any person or vehicle. We had this information from the lips of two of the oldest inhabitants of the town, both of whom have taken part in the custom, and whose veracity is unimpeachable" (*History of Fordingbridge*, by Reginald Hannen, 1883).

FRITHAM is a hamlet belonging to the parish of Bramshaw, surrounded by the finest woodland scenery of this area.

GODSHILL WOOD. Planted in 1810. Oak and Scots pine with holly undergrowth, much of which has been cut during the 1914-18 war, leaving spacious fern-grown vistas that now add to the beauty of the wood. At the Western end of the wood there is an outlying bluff, overlooking the Avon, called "Castle Hill," which is fortified by earthworks that appear to belong to the Norman period. A mile distant from Godshill Wood, to the South, on the edge of a wooded scarp that falls abruptly down to the Avon, stands Frankenbury, the largest British camp of defence in the Forest district.

The Northern end of Godshill Wood is bounded by a grassy, deep-rutted track, running West to East, that separates it from Densome, or Densham Wood. There is local tradition that this was the old way along which Cranborne Chase wheat was carried to Southampton; and the Court Rolls of the Hundred of Ford (1834), support such tradition of an ancient way in the following presentment : "We present that every person going through Densham Wood except by ancient path shall forfeit for every offence five shillings."

HASLEY. Planted in 1846. Scots pine, larch, oak and sweet chestnut. On the Northern side of the enclosure the sandy soil is stained orange by iron, and limonite iron-stone occurs, which may account for the old diggings on the North-Eastern side. The Roman potters knew the fire-resisting nature of heath-stone, or iron-stone (sand indurated with iron), and used it

Moyles Court.

33

in their kiln constructions near by. This may have been their quarry.

HOLLY HATCH. Planted in 1808. Oak and Scots pine. The word "hatch" indicates that a hatch gate stood here. cf. Hatchet Green, Hale, and Hatchet Pond, Beaulieu.

ISLANDS THORNS. Planted in 1850. Oak, larch and Scots pine. There is a Roman pottery site here, where sherds of "New Forest" pottery may be found showing finer quality and more variety of ware than at Sloden.

KING'S GARN. Planted in 1860. Near here the Bracklesham clay beds are full of fossil shells, which are described in Wise's *New Forest* and in the Hampshire Field Club Proceedings, 1885, by J. W. Elwes. They are bedded in grey-blue clay, and beautifully preserved.

LATCHMORE is the most spacious bottom in this area. It is covered with heather, furze-brakes, and thickets of holly and thorn, through which a brook flows at will down Latchmore bottom, now rippling over flats of flood-washed gravel, now oozing through marshes of sedge, sweet-gale and bog-bean, now cutting its channel in fantastic loops through grassy lawns. Scattered ponies and cattle feed over this expanse, or congregate in times of summer heat around the shallow pool known as Latchmore "shade." In autumn fern-carts labour along the deep-rutted tracks that intersect the bottom, otherwise there is little coming or going here. Time's changes have left Latchmore untouched, and it is typical of the prospect that the open Forest must have presented for centuries past.

A rough track leads up the bottom from Ogdens to Fritham.

The place-name *Latchmore* also occurs at the Northern extremity of Setley plain. (*Laece, Lache, Latch*, Old English, a stream through a bog.)

34

LINWOOD is a hamlet belonging to Ellingham parish. There are Roman pottery sites on, and near Black Heath meadow, where coarse ware was made of similar type to the Sloden ware. I have excavated two undisturbed kilns here, and found one coin of Licinius I, A.D. 307, which gives an indication of the date of this pottery site.

MILKHAM. Planted in 1861. Scots pine, most of which were cut during the 1914-18 war. After the lapse of six years a few Scots pine and oak self-sown seedlings are growing up, but no birch.

MOYLES COURT stands beside Dockenswater on the verge of Rockford common and outside the Forest Boundary, but so near that we may be allowed to overstep our limits in order to include this historic site. Moyles Court was first so called in 1392. *Moyles*, from the family of Meoles, or Meoles, who held this manor in the 14th century. *Court* probably from the Court Baron, incident to the manor, being held here. It is built of red brick, with hipped gables to its tiled roof, projecting eaves, and great chimney-stacks. It may have been built in the reign of Charles II. The South wing and the stables retain the character of this period. There is a wood-cut of Moyles Court in the *Gentleman's Magazine* 1828, which shows a large wing, now pulled down, on the West of the existing building.

The execution of Dame Alicia Lisle is the historical tragedy connected with Moyles Court. At the time of the Duke of Monmouth's rebellion against James II, 1685, Dame Alicia Lisle was an old lady of seventy, living in retirement, the widow of William Lisle, a Roundhead who had been proscribed by the Parliament of Charles II, and who was assassinated in Switzerland, 1664. She and her son were Royalists. So the tragedies of a crime, and of a divided house, had then over-shadowed the family of Lisle at Moyles Court. After the failure of Monmouth's rebellion and his capture near Horton Common (five miles distant), Dame Alicia sheltered two of his adherents, Hicks and Nelthorpe, who were arrested at Moyles Court by the King's troops. For thus giving them shelter Dame Alicia was tried before Judge Jeffreys at Winchester ; she was acquitted by the jury who, however, overawed by Jeffreys, subsequently reversed their own verdict, and thus enabled him to condemn Dame Alicia to be burnt. The King "of his clemency" commuted this sentence from the stake to the axe, and so this venerable lady was beheaded in the Square at Winchester. Her tomb stands in Ellingham churchyard, thus inscribed :

"Here lies Dame Alicia Lisle
and her Daughter Ann Harfell
who Dyed the 17 of February 1702
Alicia Lisle Dyed the
second of September 1685."

Near Moyles Court, on the South side of Dockenswater, stands the finest oak in the district. Wise, writing in 1860, states that its girth measured eighteen feet eight and a half inches, but he does not state at what height his measurement was taken. I measured this oak in 1902 at four feet from the ground, and recorded its girth as being nineteen feet eight inches and again in 1921 at the same height as being twenty feet four inches. Measurements of gnarled trees, standing on uneven ground, are liable to vary, but it seems that this oak has increased its girth since 1860. The longest lateral spread of branch is on the North-Western side, namely fifty-five feet from the trunk to the outermost twigs. Now, 1923, this old tree seems to be failing, judging from its extremities.

OCKNELL. Planted in 1775. A beautiful wood of oak and beech with holly undergrowth, channelled by the head springs of Highland water. On the Northern side of the wood stands a clump of Scots pines which was probably then planted as an experiment, to see if this "foreign" tree would thrive in New Forest soil. It seems to have completely died out in this part of England, but the remains of submerged forests found in making Southampton docks show that it was indigenous in prehistoric times. (See page 73.)

Ocknell Pond is on the summit of the plain, three hundred and sixty feet above the sea on the North-West side of the wood. It is a natural "mist" pond, solely dependent for its supply on rainfall and mist. In times of drought it rarely gives out, but in 1911 it was quite dry, for the first time in fifty years, and yet again in 1921. Its circuit is three hundred and seventeen paces, its greatest depth about two feet, and it is encircled by grassy lawns where ponies and cattle come to "shade" in summer when the woods and valleys are unbearably hot. A clay and "callous" (gravelstone indurated with iron) floor retains the surface water, and when the wind blows across the exposed plain the lapping waves crumble the surrounding banks of sandy clay; their erosion suggests the gradual making of Ocknell Pond as we now see it. Janesmoor Pond, Longcross Pond nearby, and Hatchet Pond on Beaulieu heath appear to have been made by similar action. (cf. Richardson's Map of the New Forest, 1789, for the contours of Hatchet Pond at that date.)

PICKED POST is about three miles from Ringwood on the highroad to Cadnam, and marks the summit of one of the gravel bluffs that flank the Forest side of the Avon valley. The view from here is very extensive. This place is now usually spelt "Picket," because, it is said, a picket of soldiers was posted here to suppress the smugglers who used "smugglers' road," leading into the Forest from Crow, hence the Picket Post place-name. If so, we should expect to find such spelling when the above supposed origin of the name was in recent remembrance. But we do not. It was then spelt 'Picked'; see Richardson King and Driver's *Map of the New Forest*, 1789. Gilpin's *Forest Scenery* (map) 1794. J. Cary's *Map of Hampshire*, 1801. *Cary's New Itinerary* (road book), 1802. Percival Lewis' *Topographical Remarks on the New Forest* (map), 1811. Ordnance Survey *Map of Hampshire*, 1817. Bullar's *Tour Round Southampton* (map), 1819; and finally this spelling was endorsed by J. R. Wise, *The New Forest* (map), 1863. The name probably referred to the pointed angle of the roads that join here where a post stood. *Picked* is a Wessex word in present use, meaning *pointed*. "*Picked piece*," and "*Picked rough*," constantly occur as names for triangular fields. *Picket corner* is marked in the modern Ordnance Survey maps at the Northern end of Studley, near Bramshaw Telegraph; this also appears to be a *Picked* place-name, applying to the pointed corner of the wood.

PINNICK AND REDSHOOT are fine old woods of oak, thorn and holly, with scattered crab-apple trees, growing on the stiff clay hillsides that flank Greenford Bottom. Linford brook flows through this bottom, and access to Pinnick is generally more or less waterlogged. Pinnick is crowded with self-sown seedling trees which form continuous thickets overshadowed here and there by old oaks of contorted growth. Redshoot is less crowded, the old trees are of finer growth, and they stand amid glades of bracken that slope down to Greenford Bottom. Daffodils, columbines, and butterfly orchises grow hereabouts, and those may benefit who knows where, and when, to seek therefor; but remember "picking and stealing" are conjoined! The sight of wild flowers growing and blowing is a delightful vision —not to be enhanced, in remembrance, by watching blooms wilting in a vase. Picking, however, does seem to fulfil a human requirement. Pick, if you must—but don't uproot. That *is* stealing.

A Forest track leads along the Redshoot ridge from Broomy to Highwood and Linford. *Red*, here, perhaps marks the colour of the clay soil. *Shoot*, from French *shute*, a steep, inclined plane, is a common Forest place-name suffix for a hillside track, e.g. *Whiteshoot*, which occurs frequently, the prefix marks the colour of the top-spit gravel stones, bleached by the acids from the heath roots.

RINGWOOD stands outside the Forest Boundary, but there is a Forest tradition relating to the sign of the White Hart in Ringwood, which is thus recorded in *Notes and Queries*—"It appears the King (Henry VII), accompanied by several lords of the Court, Philip, Archduke of Spain, Joan his wife, and many other ladies feeling disposed for a day's hunting, repaired to the New Forest for that purpose. A celebrated White Hart, called Albert, showed them some fine running, and the chase continued till nearly the close of day, when at length being hard pressed by the hounds, he crossed a river near Ringwood, and finally stood at bay in a meadow. His pursuers came up just as the hounds were about to make a sacrifice of their victim, when the ladies interfered for the noble animal who had given them such a fine day's sport. In answer to their prayers the hounds were called off and the animal secured. He was taken to Ringwood, and a gold collar being placed round his neck, he was removed to Windsor, while Halliday Wagstaffe (keeper of the woods and Forests in the reign of Henry VII), was that day knighted in Ringwood. The house of entertainment, at which the King and his courtiers partook of some refreshment, had its sign altered to that of the White Hart, and it has retained its name to this day ; the old signboard was taken down, and a splendid painting of a white hart, with a gold collar round its neck, supplied its place, which illustration remained till within our recollection." (The signname of this "house of entertainment" remains, but the "illustration" is wanting.)

ROE WOOD. Planted in 1811. Oak with occasional sweet chestnut and Scots pine, and thorn undergrowth. The chestnuts have grown much better than the oaks. Castlepiece, Roe, is a circular pre-Roman camp of defence, much concealed by trees. A Forest track leads through the wood from Linwood to the Ringwood and Cadnam highroad.

RUFUS' STONE stands in the Canterton Valley below Stony Cross, surrounded by beautiful old beech woods; it marks the place where, according to tradition, William Rufus was killed, 1100 A.D. Chroniclers are either silent, or give different versions as to how it happened, but agree in regarding his violent end as a just punishment for evil-doing. The tradition that has survived is recorded below. Tyrell's ford near Avon is said to have been thus named because it was crossed by Walter Tyrell in his flight after the fatal event. The name Purkis or Purkiss still survives in the county. The stone has been enclosed by a three-sided cast-iron case bearing the following record in raised letters:

1

"HERE STOOD THE OAK TREE, ON WHICH AN ARROW, SHOT BY SIR WALTER TYRELL AT A STAG, GLANCED, AND STRUCK KING WILLIAM THE SECOND, SURNAMED RUFUS, ON THE BREAST, OF WHICH STROKE HE INSTANTLY DIED, ON THE 2ND OF AUGUST, 1100.

2

"KING WILLIAM THE SECOND, SURNAMED RUFUS, BEING SLAIN AS BEFORE RELATED, WAS LAID IN A CART

BELONGING TO ONE PURKIS AND DRAWN FROM THENCE TO
WINCHESTER, AND BURIED IN THE CATHEDRAL CHURCH OF
THAT CITY.

3

"THAT THE SPOT WHERE AN EVENT SO MEMORABLE
(SIC) MIGHT NOT HEREAFTER BE FORGOTTEN, THE
ENCLOSED STONE WAS SET UP BY JOHN LORD DELAWARE,
WHO HAD SEEN THE TREE GROWING IN THIS PLACE.

"THIS STONE HAVING BEEN MUCH MUTILATED, AND
THE INSCRIPTIONS ON EACH OF ITS THREE SIDES DEFACED,
THIS MORE DURABLE MEMORIAL, WITH THE ORIGINAL
INSCRIPTIONS, WAS ERECTED IN THE YEAR 1841, BY
WILLIAM STURGES BOURNE, WARDEN."

'Happened' is the missing word in 3 above (see
Remarks on Forest Scenery by William Gilpin, vol. I,
p. 166, Ed. of 1794). Anyone who has had to deal with
inscriptions will know that tendency to error lies in wait
to confound the inscriber, as here. Even this omission
has a variant! (see Gough's Edition of Camden's
Britannia, vol. I, p. 131—'had happened.'

SLODEN is an old wood of great variety, oak, ash,
yew, whitebeam, crab-apple, holly and thorn; with
"ivy drums" clasping old trunks, and branching aloft
to find a place in the sun for their glossy foliage. Anses
has been claimed as the most beautiful valley-wood
of this area, now Sloden shall be claimed as the most
beautifully wooded hillside, both in respect of the lie
of the land, and of the growth and contrast in foliage
of the trees that crown the hill. Nowhere in the Forest
do yews and whitebeams grow in such profusion.

SLODEN ENCLOSURE. Planted in 1864. Oak,
ash and Scots pine, with a few well-grown Douglas and
Silver firs. On the six inch sheet of the Ordnance
Survey there is inscribed within this enclosure: "sup-

41

posed site of the Ancient Town of SLODEN." For "Town," we shall be nearer the mark if we read "tun" (homestead), i.e., the homesteds of the Roman potters who worked here, and have left earthwork traces of their pastoral enclosure. Their kilns were scattered over a large area ; six separate sites may be found here, over-grown with nettles, and with occasional tutsan (both unusual undergrowth), littered with Roman pottery sherds, and black, burnt earth upturned by rabbit scrapes. By kind permission of Mr. V. F. Leese, I have recently excavated four undisturbed kilns here. They were made of puddled clay that became terra cotta beneath the action of fire, and their planning indicated the "Romanisation" of their makers. Three perfect vessels, which are now in the British Museum, were found in these excavations, but no coins. Perhaps barter was the medium of exchange between these potters and their customers, pottery for wheat, which would account for the lack of coins. Anyhow, they had no lack of customers, and New Forest ware is found on excavated Roman sites throughout Britain. Their period of active production seems to have culminated A.D. 250-350. (cf. "Roman Pottery kilns at Sloden, etc." by the author). The pottery they made at Sloden was of a coarser, earlier type than that made at Crock Hill, Islands Thorns or Ashley Rails. A Forest track leads along the ridge from Fritham to Ogdens.

SLUFTERS. Planted in 1862. Scots pine, much of which has been cut during the 1914-18 war, with some well-grown Douglas firs near the high-road.

STONY CROSS is a hamlet belonging to the parish of Minstead, consisting of the "Compton Arms" hotel, and a few detached houses nearby. It stands on a plateau gravel ridge three hundred and sixty-nine feet above the sea, commanding spacious prospects on all sides. Stony Cross and Picked Post may claim to

Moyles Court Oak.

have the finest air, and the finest views, of any inhabited sites in the Forest. The Cross marks the intersection of the road from Ringwood to Romsey with the road from Lyndhurst to Downton. Stony, or Stoney? Both spellings have the sanction of local print, cf. Pony or Poney. The latter, old-fashioned. There is no meaning at issue in such variant spellings, as there is in *Picket* and *Picked*.

WOOD GREEN is a beautifully situated village at the extreme North-Western corner of the Forest. Here, for about a mile, the Avon flows as the Forest boundary, below the wooded bluff of Castle Hill before mentioned. It lies on gravel, sloping West, and faces a fine view across the Avon valley to the chalk of Cranborne Chase. Merry trees (black cherries), and orchards abound here, and the cottage gardens vie with those at Breamore as the gayest in the district.

CHAPTER FOUR

★

The Middle Area

Headquarters : *Lyndhurst, Brockenhurst, Burley, Stony Cross.*
Landmarks : *Lyndhurst church spire, Puckpits, Bolder-wood firs, Burley Beacon, Wilverley.*

THE main feature of this area is woodland. Old woods in all stages of maturity and decay. Enclosures of young trees. Thickets of undergrowth. Woods that seem to be interminable. Excepting heathland that stretches from Brockenhurst to Thorny Hill, to Burley, and thence on to Bratley plain, and excepting cultivated land around Lyndhurst, Minstead and Burley, the roads that traverse the Middle area, East, West, North, or South, pass through continuous woods. Planted woods. Probably there are far more trees in the Forest now than when William the Conqueror claimed it.

The pedestrian will explore here to the best advantage, either by seeking the old woods wherever lofty trees may be seen rising above young trees ; or by following up the courses of Highland water, Bratley water, or Ober water, which will lead him by devious, lonely ways, through great woods to upland moors whence their sources issue. Every time of year has its own especial beauty. Winter reveals lichens that

45

grow like grey fur on bare branches, mosses that clothe boles and limbs with vivid green, buds that show subtle difference of colour such as can only be seen in a smokeless district, and moorlands clad in sober vesture of dun brown. In spring the tender green of young leaves contrasts with the ruddy buds of backward beeches, the golden furze-brakes with the silver bloom of thorns and crab-apples, the rust-coloured catkins of sweet-gale with the withered bog-sedge. In summer the old woods are in heavy foliage, the thickets are wreathed with honeysuckle and crowded with bracken and foxgloves breast-high; the heather is in bloom, and the bogs are starred with cotton-grass and gilded with asphodel. So the year waxes, and then wanes; until woods, heaths, and bogs assume their final splendour of autumn colouring; but whatever the season the Forest vegetation bestows its fullest beauty of colour when it is wet. Of these seasons, summer is my last choice, because the Forest streams are then reduced to trickling shallows and stagnants pools and because a plague of flies then torments both man and beast. But at all times of the year, the first things needful for progress through the Forest is that the pilgrim should be well shod, for here he must always reckon with bogs and waterlogged bottoms.

What is the age of the trees in the old woods? Such question is inevitable. An approximate answer can be given if we take the old trees in Ridley wood as our standard for comparison. They are mostly beeches, past prime, that extend lofty, multiple limbs from gnarled, pollarded stems; and we know when they were pollarded. Thus, the underwood of "Encoppicements," as planted enclosures were called in the 15th and 16th centuries, used to be leased to tenants, who sometimes exceeded their rights. An indictment is recorded in a presentment of the regarders of the Forest relating

46

to the tenant of Ridley "coppice" in 1571, for "shrouding (pollarding) two hundred trees in the said wood and selling the same." Accordingly these trees were pollarded three hundred and fifty-three years ago, at which time they were big enough to be regarded as "trees," and may have been planted after the passing of Henry VIII's Statute of Woods, 1543 ; so we may suppose them to be now about three hundred and eighty years old. Such like pollard trees, both oaks and beeches, will be found in all the old woods, and they may be compared with these datable pollards in Ridley Wood. It is probable that the life of a tree is prolonged by pollarding. Certainly the trees thus "shrouded," and then left to grow freely, are some of the most beautiful trees in the Forest. We have no cause to complain of illegal acts committed in the 16th century. (cf. *Arboriculture of the New Forest*, by the Hon. Gerald Lascelles).

Ridley Wood also supplies evidence of the protective method of enclosure employed by the mediaeval tree-planter. This old wood is still surrounded by a wasted bank and ditch, on which, and outside which, fine self-sown trees now grow. We know that in 1571 a fence stood on this bank, because the regarders also then indicted the said tenant for "divers and many young oaks felled for stakes for the hedge." Protection by bank, ditch and "hedge" (fence) ; varied tree-planting ; natural regeneration by the up-growth of self-sown seedling trees ; and the chances of Time ; have all helped to produce the old woods that we now seek and admire, but we cannot look forward to such ultimate beauty arising from enclosures that protect pure woods of Scots pine.

The care and cultivation of woodlands appear to have been practised for centuries before Ridley "coppice" was planted, even before the date of Domesday (1085-6), for it records the measurements of woods, their capacity for yielding profit, their different kind of growth, and the number of swine which their pannage (fallen mast of oak and beech trees), would support. The following terms used in Domesday define different kinds of wood-land growth, and seem to indicate the practice of forestry then existing : *Silva*, timber trees bearing mast. *Silva infructuosa*, not bearing mast. *Silva modica*, immature. *Silva minuta, and Silva parva*, underwood. *Broca*, brushwood. *Spinetum*, thorn. The prevalence of old beeches in the Forest represents survival of pannage purpose in tree-planting, while the comparative rarity of old oaks is due to constant demand for navy timber during past centuries.

In times past the Forest high-roads, running straight across heathlands and through woodlands added beauty to the scene. The yellow road belonged to the soil, as the roadside gravel-pits testified, and when the sun was low these golden roads were barred with blue-purple shadows that gave mystery to the passage of the high-way. Now, such old-fashioned roads are being super-seded by granite, tarred tracks of dull slate colour, whereon black shadows lie, and gravel, as high-road metal, will soon be only a memory.

Deer may often be seen in the great woods of the Middle area.

PLACES OF INTEREST

ALDRIDGE HILL. Planted in 1775 and 1809. A re-enclosed wood of well-grown oaks, which have been thinned, and are now surrounded by young plants of oak and occasional beech, sweet chestnut, and birch. Aldridge Hill and Rhinefield Sandy nearby (also planted in 1775), are good examples of the cultivation of trees by natural regeneration.

BACKLEY ENCLOSURE. Planted in 1829, mostly sweet chestnut, the mast of which is sought after and gathered in the autumn. The sweet chestnut is supposed to have been introduced into Britain by the Romans. "There is mention made in a New Forest account roll, *temp.* Edward III, of a chestnut wood (bosco de castaneariis)." cf. *The Royal Forests of England*, by Dr. Cox. There is little planting of chestnuts done nowadays. Its timber after about sixty years growth is apt to become "shaky," but if cut young, it is as durable as oak for posts and piles, and its wood is almost all spine. The supposed use of chestnut timber for old roofs appears to have been founded on wrong identification; the wood of the sessile fruited oak having been mistaken for that of the chestnut. cf. *Arboretum et Fruticetum*, by J. C. Loudon, vol. III, p. 1989.

BERRY BEECHES; not pollarded; crown the ridge that leads from Burley moor to Backley Plain, and are specially fine on the Eastern slopes of the ridge; they are remarkable both for their beauty and for the curious examples of ingrowth shown in their stems and branches. Vipers are said to abound on this ridge. Referring to snakes, those that frequent the Western side of the Forest, are grass snakes, vipers, and the smooth snake (Coronella Laevis, or Coluber Austriacus), first identified in 1853 at Parley Heath, near Wimborne. Its British habitat appears to be confined to the Western heathlands of the New Forest, and to those of Dorset adjoining. cf. *On Coronella Laevis*, by Rev. O. Pickard Cambridge. Dorset Field Club Transactions. Vol. III. There is great variety in the colour of vipers in the Forest, from silvery grey with black zigzag markings, to buff, to reddish, with brown markings.

BOLDERWOOD LODGE used to be a residence occupied by a "master keeper," but without salary or duties, the work being done by "groom keepers." It was occupied by Lord de la Warr in 1732, added to in 1747, and pulled down in 1833. The Lodge stood near the present-day keeper's cottage. Traces of the extensive grounds remain, and within them stand the tall silver firs that are landmarks of Bolderwood from afar. About sixty years ago many sorts of conifers were planted here, of which Douglas firs are now specially remarkable for their luxuriant growth.

BROCKENHURST is a large village amid beautiful Forest surroundings, which has grown rapidly in recent times owing to its excellent train service. The church is ancient, parts of its fabric date from mid 12th century, and additions were made in the 13th and 14th centuries. The circular platform mound on which it stands is remarkable, and arouses curious questionings as to its origin. There is an ancient, free-grown yew on the South side of the West end, of which Sir Daniel Morris says : "The girth of this tree when I measured it in October, 1915, was eighteen feet four inches, the height about sixty feet, while the diameter of the ground covered by the branches was seventy feet." (Presidential Address to Bournemouth Natural Science Society, 1915). The church mentioned in Domesday at "Broceste" appears subsequently to have become a chapelry dependent upon Boldre (Vict. Hist. of Hampshire, vol. IV, p. 629). "Broceste, here is a church," and "church land at Melleford" (Milford), are the only references to churches in Domesday New Forest Survey.

Balmer Lawn, Setley Plain, Hinchesley, Rhinefield and Queen's Bower are place-names that may recall the varied scenery to be found near Brockenhurst. The old oaks along the course of the stream in Queen's Bower are specially characteristic of the growth of these trees in the Forest. "They do not grow to any considerable height, as oaks usually do in richer soils, but rather

Mark Ash.

51

extend their branches horizontally, and in most irregular forms : the consequence that results from it is that the timber is more particularly adapted to what shipbuilders term knees and elbows, and on that account becomes more valuable." Times have changed since the above was written by Percival Lewis in 1811, and oak no longer rules the wave, but his description of these old trees still holds good.

BURLEY is also a growing place. Owing to land sales there has been much new building here recently. It was an extra parochial hamlet of smallholders surrounding Burley Manor : it is a large village with many residential houses, big and little, added to its former state of occupation. Such growth has changed the character of Burley, but has not destroyed its essential Forest charm. Woods, moors, and lawns still surround, enter, and intersect this scattered village in every direction.

Castle Hill is a pre-Roman camp of defence at the Northern end of Burley Beacon ridge. There is a fine view from here over the Avon valley, Dorset, and Wiltshire. Below the entrenched camp ran a Saxon "here-path" (war-path), along the line of road from Burley to Ringwood. Saxon herepaths usually followed the traffic lines of previous origin, which suggests the antiquity of this way.

There is a legend attached to Burley Beacon, which is recorded in the Victoria History of Hampshire, vol. IV, p. 609. "A document at Berkeley Castle, of a date earlier than 1618," tells the story.

"Sir Morls Barkley the sonne of Sir John Barkley, of Beverston, beinge a man of great strength and courage, in his tyme there was bread in Hampshire neere Bisterne a devouring Dragon, who doing much mischief upon men and cattel and could not be destroyed but spoiled many in attempting it, making his den neere unto a Beacon. This Sir Moris Barkley armed himself and encountered with it and at length overcam and killed it but died himself soone after." . . . (Sir Maurice Berkeley was the son of Sir John Berkeley and of Elizabeth de Bettesthorne, Bisterne, and died in 1460).

There used to be a "Green Dragon" Inn, nearly opposite the school at Bisterne : and there are two "Dragon Fields" in the Bisterne estate. The "Green Dragon" Inn sign at Brook probably refers to this legend, for the redoubtable "Sir Moris Barkley" was also Lord of the Manor of Minstead and Brook in right of his mother; so local place-names attest mediaeval popular acceptance of this wild legend.

Burley rock is the name given to stone which has been dug on Rock Hill (near Markway Hill), and on the ridge near Bisterne Close Farm. It is a conglomerate of gravel-stones and sand indurated with iron, a durable impervious, intractable material of dull rust colour, used nowadays for foundations, rough walling, and rockeries.

Burley Lodge stands in the midst of the great woods, near the road from Burley to Lyndhurst. It was occupied by the Dukes of Bolton from about 1700 to 1809. The old Lodge has been pulled down. There used to be a group of old oaks standing in the grounds adjoining that were known as the Twelve Apostles, of which few now remain.

BUSHY BRATLEY is a famous old wood standing above Bratley water, to the East of the Ringwood and Cadnam highroad. These venerable beeches are now in a stage of gradual decay. Gaps and clearances occur in the wood. Here, the ruin of an uprooted tree, there, piles of cord-wood amid crowds of foxgloves, telling of latter-day windfalls, and of "sign (assigned) wood" awaiting clearance. And we cannot console ourselves with good hope for the future. There is not much chance for natural regeneration in Bushy Bratley, because there are few thickets here to protect young seedling trees from the destructive nibbling of Forest cattle and ponies.

The distant view of Bushy Bratley from Mogshade Hill, on the way from Lyndhurst to Ringwood, is a vision that haunts one's mind's eye. The old trees rising eminent in massed verdure—the irregular verge of self-sown beeches, making shadowy bays and sunlit promontories of foliage, the surrounding stretches of fern brake and heather, and Bratley water below, meandering through thickets.

EMERY DOWN is a residential district, half a mile distant from Lyndhurst to the North West. The sudden rise and fall of the land here, and the medley of buildings, gardens, orchards and forest give special charm to the village. "St. James' Hill" (place-name in six inch ordnance survey map) was named "Gravel Hill" in 1789 according to Richardson King and Driver's map. Old gravel-diggings on the top surface of the hill testify to the name. This abrupt mount, three hundred feet above the sea, is a curious example of an outlying, isolated hill of which the gravel-capping has resisted sub-aerial denudation.

HIGHLAND WATER ENCLOSURE. Planted 1869. Scots pine, cut down during the 1914-18 war, thereby improving the wide prospect of Mogshade Hill. The folds of the hillside descending to Highland water, make a fine, broken foreground to woods below, with the grove of old trees at Puckpits marking the summit of the hill opposite, while Southward the view extends across Southampton Water, and its adjacent lowlands, to the distant South downs and Spithead. Mogshade Hill used to be covered with beautiful thickets of old holly trees, now, alas, badly burnt by a recent (1918) fire, which is remembered as a wartime, careless mishap, to the discredit of overseas woodmen.

HINCHESLEY. Domesday entry. "Wislac held half a hide in Hincelveslei ; and it was assessed at that quantity. It is now in the Forest. There is land for two ploughs. It was worth twenty shillings."

The present-day residence at Hinchesley stands at the end of an outlying spur of Wilverley Plain, flanked on the North by Redhill and Holmhill bogs, and on the South by Long Slade Bottom. The lie of the land, and the adjoining soil indicate that present-day occupation probably corresponds with Wislac's holding of about sixty acres in A.D. 1086. The well-wooded knoll of Hinchesley is a feature in the landscape, as seen from the low-lying expanses of Rhinefield Walk, or from the Southern Railway to Weymouth, although in height it does not rise to the two hundred feet line.

HOLMSLEY ENCLOSURE. Planted in 1811. Oak and Scots pine. Holmsley bog and the Avon water valley are natural preserves for the botanist. Thorny Hill Holms nearby, are dense groves of hollies that fringe the Forest Boundary at Thorny Hill "Devil's Den" (*Divell's Den*. Perambulation of 1681. *Develdon*. Perambulation of 1301) is now unknown as a place-name, but a track through the Holms is known as "Devil's Walk."

KNIGHTWOOD OAK stands near the Lyndhurst and Bournemouth high-road, beside Knightwood Enclosure (planted 1867 cut down during the 1914-18 war). It is a fine pollard in vigorous old age, and is protected by an encircling spiked-pale fence. J. R. Wise, in 1862, records its girth as being seventeen feet four inches. W. F. Ransly, in 1906, "nearly nineteen feet at four feet from the ground." The Rev. C. Darling, in 1921, twenty-one feet six inches, at the same height.

LYNDHURST, from its position, traditions, and

surroundings is the capital of the New Forest District. It is situated in the midst of the Forest; the King's House is the centre of the Forest administration; and it is surrounded by some of the most beautiful woodland and moorland scenery in the Forest.

The finest approach to Lyndhurst is along the road from Christchurch, past Warwick Slade, across Highland water, under green canopies of beech foliage, spreading from Gritnam on the right and Bramble Hill on the left, through the lawns of Allum Green haunted by commoners' stock, up and down the wooded knoll of Bank, and then, the Forest ends abruptly, tradesmen's cars ply, and behold, a prosperous little country town. It would be difficult to find a similar change of scene within a mile, so quick, and so complete.

Lyndhurst's present claim as the capital of the Forest, was not ecclesiastically recognised in the past. It is a chapelry attached to the church at Minstead. The present church was built in 1863 on the site of an old chapel described in the reign of Edward I as attached to our lodgings at Lyndhurst." It contains a fresco by Sir Frederick Leighton on the chancel East wall, and an early example of William Morris' stained-glass windows.

The King's House, which stands on the Western side of the church, was the manor house of the Royal manor of Lyndhurst. It dates for the most part from 1634, and the Verderer's Hall adjoining from 1388, but the latter has undergone much alteration. Over the fireplace of this hall hangs the so-called "stirrup of Rufus," which is traditionally supposed to have been the test for such dogs as might be kept free in the Forest. If a dog was sufficiently small to pass through this stirrup, it was accounted free from "expedition" (see page 95).

The last Justice Seat for the Forest was held here

in 1669-70.

MALWOOD CASTLE is the site of a small pre-Roman camp of defence. There is no evidence in support of the tradition that a Norman castle once stood here. Castle place-names connected with ancient earthworks occur on this side of the Forest. For example, Castle Hill Burley, and Castle Piece Roe Wood (pre-Roman camps of defence). Lucas' Castle (a hill above Highland water near Ocknell). Studley Castle (a small pastoral earthwork near Bramshaw Telegraph). Thompson's Castle (a barrow on Latchmore). Castle Hill Godshill wood is the only castle place-name that probably marks a Norman site.

There is, however, evidence, dating from 1358, that a Forest Lodge stood here, and that it was called *Hardebourgh, Herbarwe,* or *Harebergh.* Hardus Green appears to be a survival of this forgotten place-name. A private residence now occupies the site.

MARK ASH is an old wood, mostly consisting of ancient pollard and free-grown beeches in every stage of prime growth, past prime, and gradual decay (the last predominating), with an undergrowth of holly and thorn. Some of these old beeches have remarkable girth. The "Queen Beech," a pollard of beautiful growth, is eighteen feet one inch at four feet from the ground, and nearby stands a beech that divided into six vertical stems at ten feet from the ground, which shoot up thirty feet before they branch. This tree measures twenty feet eleven inches at four feet from the ground. Marked boundary-tree place-names frequently denote the limits of primitive West-Saxon settlements, e.g., Cut-thorn, Marke oak, Bound oak, etc. Possibly the name Mark Ash is older than the afforestation of William I in A.D. 1079. Anyhow, here and now, the marked boundary ash tree will be looked for in vain.

Mark Ash is reached from Lyndhurst either by the

road that skirts Bolderwood Rails, or by a good Forest track which turns into Knightwood Enclosure from the Christchurch road near Knightwood oak. It shares with Rufus' stone the penalties of popularity, but the old woods around Mark Ash are far-reaching, while the range of holidaymakers is near. Disturbance is passing and partial. Mystery amid a great company of tree abides here notwithstanding.

MINSTEAD has been less affected by the changes of time than any other village in the Forest. Its thatched cottages, flowery gardens, and old orchards are scattered along twisting roads avoided by motorists. Its brook is still unbridged and crossed by a gravelly, shallow ford. But recently (1921) there have been land sales here, and new residential conditions will arise.

The church stands upon a hill, like all the churches in the Forest, except Beaulieu, and has escaped the heavy hand of the 19th century restorer. The interior is very interesting and expressive of the past. The fabric dates from the 13th to the 18th centuries. The "Trusty Servant" Inn sign is unique in Hampshire. It dates from about 1700, and the origin of this sign is a picture outside the kitchen of Winchester College, where it is accompanied by the following verses :

"*A trusty Servant's portrait would you see*
This emblematic figure well survey;
The porker's snout not nice in diet shows,
The padlock shut no secret he'll disclose.
Patient the ass his master's rage will bear,
Swiftness in errand the stag's feet declure.
Loaden his left hand apt to labour saith,
The vest his neatness; open hand his faith.
Girt with his sword, his shield upon his arm,
Himself and master he'll protect from harm."

The road through Mark Ash.

59

NEW PARK, on the left of the highroad from Brockenhurst to Lyndhurst, is Crown property ; its name is in distinction to the Old Park of Lyndhurst—now disparked. Old Park dates from 1291. New Park is first mentioned in 1484. It was added to by Charles II in 1670 "for the preservation of our red deer, newly come out of France."

OAKLEY. Planted in 1853. Oak and Scots pine. There is an avenue of fine Douglas firs in this enclosure which shows how much their growth exceeds that of the other trees, all having been planted seventy years ago. There are two Roman pottery kiln sites here.

RIDLEY WOOD stands on the South-Eastern side of the highroad from Ringwood to Cadnam, below Picked Post. This fine old wood of pollard beeches has already been referred to, and we know its approximate age from written record (page 46). The Western side of this wood is approached by a hollow way, and there is authentic hearsay tradition that this concealed hollow was used as a meeting-place by smugglers and their local customers. "Smugglers' Road," crossing the heath from Crow, marks this line of access from the Avon valley.

SETLEY PLAIN is a gravelly expanse of heather and furze-brakes by the side of the highroad from Brockenhurst to Lymington. Three well-preserved disc barrows stand on the plain (the only examples of this type within the Forest Boundary, but there is a small disc barrow on Ibsley common just outside the Boundary). The outer earthen circles of two of these barrows intersect each other.

At the Northern end of Setley Plain, amongst scattered trees and thickets, gipsies pitch their primitive tents, surrounded by the ramshackle details of their daily life. Gipsy camps, but on a smaller scale, may also generally be found at Wood Green, along the South side of Godshill wood, at Crock Hill, Cadnam Common, at Verley, and at Thorny Hill. Selling "daffies" at Bournemouth and Salisbury, and, locally, selling clothes-pegs, and sweeping cottage chimneys, in old-fashioned manner, by slimbing up and sweeping down, are the sources of their livelihood that I have come cross. Doctors tell me that they are trustworthy patients, but that their tents, inside, are impossible for diagnosis. Parsons, that they favour the church, rather than the chapel, in crises, such as marriage, birth, or death. Their ways of life are persistently aloof from present-day civilisation. Curious survivals, customary, and perhaps racial, may await discovery by a qualified observer of these gipsy settlements.

VINNEY RIDGE is crossed by the highroad from Lyndhurst to Christchurch, and is crowned with old beeches whose tree-tops used to sway beneath nesting herons, but now this heronry is deserted. In 1861 Wise says there were fifty nests here, and also a few at Bolder-wood. The only herons that may now be seen in the Forest come from the heronries at Sowley Pond, Hinton Admiral, Heron Court, or Somerly, all of which places are outside, but near the Forest Boundary.

From Vinney Ridge to Rhinefield there is a road called the "ornamental ride," flanked on either side with various sorts of conifers, thujas, and rhododendrons (planted about 1850), which are interesting as examples of experimental growth in this soil, but which do not belong to Forest scenery as we know it.

WILVERLEY ENCLOSURE. Planted in 1809 (re-enclosed in 1895). Oak, with few beech, chestnut and Scots pine of same date; fern and bramble under-growth. This planting extends over all the South-Western area of the enclosure, and the rise and fall of the land give pleasant prospects over tree-tops towards the low Wootton Hills that align Avon water and

61

Wilverley bog. In 1896-7 the oak plantation in the upper part of the enclosure was cut, because the oaks were stunted and ill-grown owing to the gravelly nature of the soil there. Scots pine and larch were planted instead, and have done well; being now almost of the same height as that of the remnants left standing of the 1809 oak plantation. There are two nurseries in this enclosure.

Outside Wilverley enclosure, on the North-Eastern side runs the road from Burley to Lymington. Here, a quarter of a mile from Wilverley Post, stands on the open heath a bare, riven oak trunk with three broken, bare limbs. "Naked Man," by place-name. Seen from the Eastern side it tells as a trunk with two arms, and it appears to have looked thus one hundred and thirty-five years ago, judging by the symbol appended to "Naked Man" place-name in Richardson, King and Driver's Map of the New Forest, 1789. Yet it still stands as a wreck, shored by four spurs to resist sea winds, still a recognised landmark, and its spine wood even now repels a knife blade.

CHAPTER FIVE

★

The Southern Area

Headquarters : *Lymington, Beaulieu, Beaulieu Road, Lyndhurst Road, Lyndhurst, Brockenhurst.*
Landmarks : *Beaulieu Hilltop Firs, Woodfidley, Lyndhurst church spire.*

THIS area is bounded on the Southern side by a low-lying stretch of cultivated sea-board beside the Solent. The landward slant of "bustle-headed" trees tells of prevailing sea winds, the stream estuaries tell of neighbouring tides, and the disused salterns in marshy flats, of a sea-water industry. Here the wayfarer arrives at a natural boundary of the Forest, the Solent.

Inland, from Sway Common to Butts Ash, gravel-capped plains rise about one hundred feet above the sea, through which streams have cut their courses towards the Solent. The valleys made by these streams are clayey and well-wooded, while the gravel plains are mostly bare heathland, overgrown in places with self-sown Scots pine. Farther inland lies boggy ground extending from Hinchesley, Brockenhurst, Beaulieu Road, to Ashurst, much of which is below the fifty foot line. This low-lying area gradually rises towards the North, across the woods of Ramnor Park Hill, Denny, and Matley Ridge, towards Lyndhurst which stands behind them, on higher ground, one hundred and seventy feet above the sea.

Such are the main characteristics and distinctive zones of the Southern area.

The sea winds' mark on tree growth in this area has already been noted. There is also a difference that may be observed between natural tree growth in the lowland and uplands of the Forest. Yews and whitebeams are comparatively rare in the lowlands, but are common in the uplands. Birch are common in the lowlands, but comparatively rare in the uplands. Birch is a tree that flourishes self-sown both in this area and on the lower slopes of the Middle area. These graceful trees add a special beauty to the fringe of Forest woodlands in the early spring, when their silvery stems and wine-coloured shoots contrast with the browns and greys and moss-greens of the timber trees, and in autumn when their foliage turns to brilliant gold colour, contrasting with the russet foliage of the oaks.

The map at the beginning of the book shows the twisting line of the London and South-Western Railway (now the Southern Railway), in its passage through the lowlands of the Forest. For this we have to thank influential Forest lovers who advocated this course, and obtained their way, when the line was made in the middle of the last century, thereby saving the old woods around Lyndhurst. "Castleman's Corkscrew" was the nickname given to this twisting line years ago, Castleman being one of the "influential" (a L. & S.W.R. Director residing near Ringwood).

Railway travellers during the month of December may see the truck-loads of crimson-berried holly-tops standing in the siding of the Forest stations, and may wonder how this wintry harvest of the woods is managed. "Hollying" begins at the end of November. The holly trees are chosen and their tops cut by the woodman in each Walk. Then the smallholder who has undertaken to buy the holly in this or that Walk, cuts up the tops into "Forest faggots," for which he pays the Crown at so much per hundred, and carts them to the nearest place of despatch. This continues day by day for a fortnight. Then all the holly faggots for the London market are sent by train to Nine Elms Yard, where they are sold to retailers. In late years, the 1914-18 war, high wages, high railway freight charges, and artificial holly have "spoilt the trade," so it is said. Lopping holly trees in their prime of beauty may provoke the Forest lover, but the crop is needed, the hollies are abundant, while pollarding probably prolongs their ultimate age and results in picturesque growth.

Chance Forest fires, and rabbits, are the real enemies of holly trees, and when fires get out of hand they are disastrous in result. If sufficient beaters are available it is sometimes possible to stay a heath fire by burning a stop-track, down wind in advance of the running fire. Thus: the beaters (armed with boughs, or with self-sown seedlings of Scots pine), spread out in line a few feet apart, and each lights a fire that will intersect those on either side when they have burnt their fiery circles; thus they will burn themselves out, except on the outsides, where their flames must be kept in check, and finally beaten out when the circles are joined. Then, when the running fire reaches this stop-track, it will die out for lack of fuel. Heath should be burnt in early spring, and when it is not very dry, so that it should not burn down to its roots. If good luck thus favours the event, young grass and fern will clothe the burnt area before midsummer, and the feed will be improved. But if a fire occurs during summer drought vegetation is burnt down to its roots, and the burnt area remains charred and bare for three or four years before the heath is renewed. Blackened furze stems remain as ugly relics of a fire for a year or two, till they rot at their roots, when they are broken off and collected for fuel by neighbouring Foresters. Dodder seems to thrive on the ash left by a forest fire. New-grown heath is often smothered by the crimson threads of this curious parasite. In dealing with heath, furze and Scots pine, their abiding liability to stray firing needs to be understood and guarded against; and holiday folk should realise that castaway cigarette ends may light a raging heath fire, and that fragments of castaway glass bottles may act as burning glasses on a sunny day, thus kindling fire. Neither the Crown nor the adjacent landowners have inherited good methods of preventing forest fires from spreading. Self-sown pines and heath are allowed to grow beside the enclosures, where a broad, grassy stoptrack should be kept, for self-sown Scots pine, afire, lead up to the burning of an adjacent Scots pine enclosure. But however we may plan, and whatever precautions we may devise, chance, good or ill, must always rule the result of heath fires in times of drought, and when a high wind blows.

Beaulieu Rails, mentioned in the notes following, represents a squatter type of habitation, that is constant all along the verge of the Forest Boundary. It is undesirable either to ask (or to answer) inquisitive questions as to ownership on the Forest Boundary. Possession is nine points of the law, and we may leave it at that; but it is desirable to ask and answer questions as to "mud-walling," or "dob" of which such cottages were built throughout the New Forest District; for this traditional craft has been dying out. Mud walls should be made of sandy, clayey loam with small stones in it; and with heath, rushes, and sedge-grass, or straw, thoroughly puddled into the mass by trampling. In the best-made mud walls this was dobbed and bonded by the mud-waller with his trident mud-prong in suc-

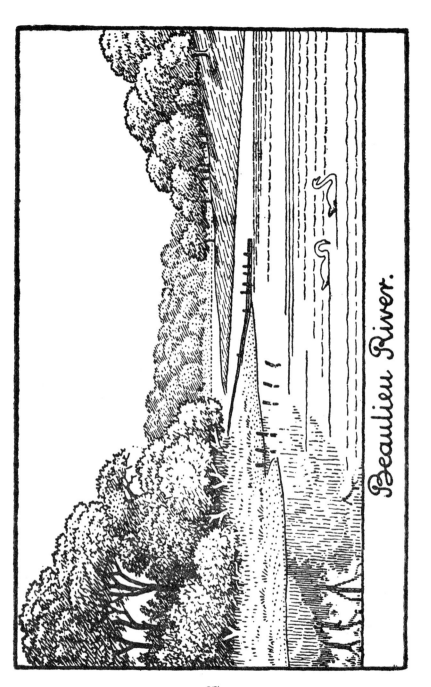

Beaulieu River.

cessive layers on the wall he was building. About two feet, vertical, being raised at a time (a "rearing"), then left for ten days to dry before the next rearing was raised on it. Walls built thus, on heathstone or brick footings, stand well. But often they were raised without any footings, and by inexperienced "mudders" who used the wrong sort of clay; who did not temper it stiff with heath; and who could not build a wall with a mud-prong, but trusted to board "clamps." and thus this serviceable walling material has been discredited; most unfairly; mud walls that have been well built stand firm and impervious for generations, and provide warmth in winter and coolness in summer within the cottages which they surround, and they cost less than walls of any other material locally available. There is excellent mud-walling still being raised, and for such requirements, I should go to Verwood; to Mr. Sims of Sutton Holms, Verwood, who has inherited the knowledge of his craft, and can point out this, that, and the other mud-walled, thatched cottage in his native village, as built by his grandfather, his father, or himself (to the last he has recently been adding). An outer-roughcast coating of plaster and pebble-dash fortifies the weatherproof nature of mud-walls, and veils a coarse material with a serviceable finish.

Local descriptive names in the Forest are sometimes curious. For example: in the lowlands near Denny, fords are called *Passages*: along the seaboard of the Southern area, from Beaulieu river to Keyhaven the channels of streams flowing through the mud flats are called *Lakoo*; while between Keyhaven and Mudeford, where streams flow down gullies to the sea, such gullies are called *Bunnys*. In the Middle area, brooks are called *Waters*. In the Northern area, *Gutters*. Throughout the Forest, tree clumps, eminent because of their growth, of because they stand on knolls, are called *Hats*. For example :

King's Hat Enclosure
Crab Hat Enclosure } Near Hartford.

Great Hat
Pigsty Hat } Near Holmsley Enclosure.

Cardinal Hat, in Holmsley Enclosure.
Bell's Hat, near Little Wootton Enclosure.

Birchen Hat
Great Birchen Hat } Near Knightwood Oak.

Great Dark Hat
Little Dark Hat } In, or near Hollidays Hill Enclosure.

Corbet's Hat, near Pilmore Heath.
King's Hat, near New Park.
Standing Hat, near Balmer Lawn.
Shave Hat, near Bartley.

Great Stubby Hat
Little Stubby Hat } Near Busketts.
Coomy Hat

Breamore Hat
Dart Hat Wood } Near Studley, Bramshaw Telegraph.

Ashen's Hat
Long Hat } Near Piper's Weight, Bramble Hill.
Black Bush Hat

The bogs in the Southern and Middle areas are the worst in the Forest, namely, Matley bog, Bishop's Ditch, Long Slade Bottom (below Hinchesley), Holmsley bog, and Bratley bog. Rakes Brakes Bottom (near Anses) and the Latchmore book in the Northern area, are also bogs to beware of; but they do not quake, and bubble, and sink so ominously beneath footfall as those aforesaid. When bogs bar the way, the wayfarer will be well advised if he circumvents the obstruction to his path.

Deer are rarely to be seen on the Southern side of the railway line : but in recent years Japanese deer have been turned out in the Beaulieu district, and are said to be thriving. They are small, about the size of roe deer.

The woods and enclosures in this area provide happy hunting grounds for entomologists.

PLACES OF INTEREST

ASHURST LODGE has been converted into a private residence. It is situated in one of the old woods near Lyndhurst Road station, on the verge of Matley Heath. There is a small, circular earthwork nearby, beside the brook that flows down Longwater Bottom, the site of which suggests pastoral shelter rather than defence as its original purpose.

BALMER LAWN is a spacious grazing ground near Brockenhurst, surrounded by an amphitheatre of woodland that rises gradually towards the North and North-East. It is the site for pony races which annually cause a complete change from the habitual, quiet forest life on Balmer Lawn.

BEAULIEU ABBEY was founded by King John in 1205 A.D., here he placed thirty Cistercian monks. He endowed the Abbey with lands, exempted it from the numerous tolls and taxes of feudal times, gave it privileges and immunities, and surrounded it with a disafforested tract of land. Forty years elapsed from the date of its foundation to that of its completion and dedication. The ceremony took place about 1246,

Henry III and his Queen being present with a great retinue. The Abbey church was larger than any belonging to the Cistercian order in England, being three hundred and thirty-six feet in length and one hundred and eighty-six feet across the transepts. Binstead stone from the Isle of Wight was used for the external work, Caen stone and Purbeck marble for the internal. "About this period (1327 A.D.) Pope Innocent received the convent of Beaulieu under the protection of the apostolical see; and by his bull, conferred on its members several great ecclesiastical privileges. Such as that of Sanctuary; an exemption from the payment of tithes; from the attendance on episcopal synods, or courts, together with a power of electing their abbot, and regulating the affairs of their convent, without the interference of the diocesan." (Warner, *Topographical Remarks*.) Thus the Beaulieu Cistercians obtained a hazardous immunity from both secular and diocesan local authority, for which they ultimately paid the penalty.

Such hazardous immunity lasted about two hundred years. Then the price was paid. Beaulieu Abbey was dissolved in 1538 A.D. Most of its buildings were pulled down, but the outer and inner gate-houses still remain, with portions of the cloisters, and of the chapter house. The Refectory also stands, and is now used as the parish church. The Abbey precincts were surrounded by a wall, parts of which still remain, and wasted earthworks indicate the site of fish stews and of ducts for water supply. The field-name of *Vineyards* confirms documentary evidence as to the monks having made their own wine here : the Cistercians were farmers as well as monks, of which we are further reminded by the remains of a noble stone barn at St. Leonards Grange (two hundred and sixteen feet long by sixty-one feet wide, standing near a 13th century chapel), by the place-name *Bergerie*, sheep farm, and *Beufre*, ox farm, and by the evidence of their constant encroachments on the Forest.

Another side of Monastic activities, for an abbot was, like Nimrod, a "mighty hunter before the Lord," is attested by the place-name *Abbotstanding* wood, on the Western side of Beaulieu river valley; a name betokening mediaeval methods of hunting. A *Stand*, *Standing*, or *Stable-stand*, was a platform, or place where shooters awaited the driven game, hidden behind a bower of branches, whence such standings were also called *ramiers*, and *folies*, from rames, or branches and folia, leaves, cf *The Master of Game*, by W. A. Baillie-Grohman. *Standing Hat*, near Balmer Lawn is another instance of a mediaeval hunting place-name.

There is an excellent description and ground plan of Beaulieu Abbey in the fourth volume of the Victoria History of Hampshire.

The site at Beaulieu, in a cultivated, wooded valley, beside the winding reaches of a tidal estuary, presents a delightful contrast to the wild heathlands adjoining. *Beautiful place* was well chosen as its name.

BEAULIEU HEATH, and BEAULIEU HILL-TOP HEATH. The wayfarer's estimate of these heaths will probably vary according to the weather that he meets with. If he chances to cross them on a wet day, when low clouds blot out the distance, and rain drifts across the plains, he will remember them as tracts of desolation. But if he chances on a fine day, when warm air quivers above the heath, and when distant views are clear, he will remember them as spacious, sunny moorlands fringed with woods, within sight of the gleaming Solent, of its shipping, and of the bare downs that dominate "the Island." Nowhere in the Forest are so many barrows, or (in local parlance) "butts," to be seen as here. Fifty-four stand on the plains of these two heaths. They suggest considerable Bronze Age occupation at a period when the land stood higher than it does now, and when the Solent may have been a fertile valley. Excavation for new docks at Southampton, circa 1889, supplied evidence of the subsidence of the valley now covered by Southampton Water. Here, twenty feet below the surface of the mud uncovered at low tide, embedded in peat, were found relics of palaeolithic and neolithic man; of handiwork—flint flakes, a round hammer stone with a worked circular hole, and a bone needle; of fauna—reindeer, wild cattle (Bos primigenius), red deer (Cervus elaphus), a small variety of horse, boar, and hare; and of flora—oak, beech, hazel, birch, and pine; bulrush, sedge, bog myrtle, heaths, and bracken.

BEAULIEU RAILS. This place-name marks a row of squatters' cottages on the Southern side of Beaulieu heath. All round the Forest Boundaries, and those of the commons adjoining, such smallholdings represent the original choice and occupation of bygone squatters.

During the 1914-18 war an aerodrome was made at the Eastern end of Beaulieu Rails.

BISHOP'S DITCH is the name given to a curiously shaped area of boggy ground, containing about five hundred acres surrounded by a rambling bank between two ditches. It is situated near Denny and Woodfidley, and is crossed by the Southern Railway, from which there is a good view of the site. Forest pasturage and sport appear to have been sought by John de Pontoise, or Pontisarra, Bishop of Winchester, when he obtained the grant of Bishop's Ditch from Edward I 1284 A.D. The area thus enclosed is now an open, low-lying, boggy waste, a favourite feeding ground of Forest ponies, intersected by runnels and shallow pools which gradually unite their flow at Pig Bush Passage and

73

become a little brook which joins the Beaulieu river. It seems probable that the present boggy condition of this area has increased since it was first enclosed. The Bishop's choice is otherwise unaccountable. The damming of the flow of Beaulieu river in later times may have caused such change. Bishop's Ditch and Matley bog, a mile distant, are examples of bogs formed under different conditions, the former lying in wide, open, converging bottoms amid expanses of heather; the latter in a narrow bottom overgrown with alders.

There is a tradition relating to this neglected enclosure, namely, that in ancient times one of the Prelates of Winchester was given as much of the Forest as he could crawl round, and that Bishop's Ditch was the result. The legend, which occurs elsewhere, seems to express country humour, attributing a fantastic origin to an unusual earthwork of which nothing was known.

BOLDRE. Boldre village is not "on the way." It is secluded, apart from the highroads leading from Lymington to Lyndhurst on one side, and to Beaulieu on the other. But its population is, comparatively, large. Its numerous cottages, small farms, and residential houses are scattered beside twisting, wooded lanes, and its church, that stands on a hill, is isolated and hidden by trees. This is a most interesting old building, dating from Norman times. There is a good coloured ground-plan in the porch, from which may be learnt the various periods of building of the church and tower. William Gilpin, a name honoured by Forest lovers, was vicar of this parish from 1771 to 1804. In his book on "Forest Scenery," he mentions a maple tree then standing in the churchyard of Boldre as one of the largest that he had seen. This tree is now in the last stage of decay. It stands on the Northern side of the church, near William Gilpin's tomb.

The stone bridge that spans the Lymington (or

The outer Gateway Beaulieu Abbey.

Boldre) river with five round arches is a notable feature in this valley scene.

It should be noted that in Richardson King and Driver's Survey Map of the New Forest, 1789, Boldre village is spelt *Bolder,* and Boldrewood—*Bolderwood.* (of also *Bolderwood Walk* p.89). In the Ordnance Survey maps, the village is spelt *Boldre,* but they follow Richardson King and Driver's spelling in *Bolderwood* and *Bolderford.* The north-western boundary of the Hundred of *Bovre* was near *Bolderwood (Boldrewood?),* and *Bolderford* suggests *Bolder (Boldre?)* as the river name.

BUCKLAND RINGS are entrenchments that defended a pre-Roman camp. This is the finest earthwork in the Forest District, for although it stands just outside the Forest Boundary it may be claimed as within the District. It stands on a bluff on the Western side of the Lymington river, and is squarish in shape. The Northern and Southern sides are defended by well-preserved triple ramparts and ditches. On the Western side a road appears to have cut into the entrenchments, and only two ramparts and one ditch remain. The entrance was on the Eastern side, and here the ramparts and ditches have been almost obliterated under cultivation. Elsewhere the trees which conceal the entrenchments have also protected and preserved them. The area of this camp contains about seven acres.

Down below in the valley, beside the Passford brook and the Lymington river, is Ampress, a small camp of which the area is now occupied by waterworks and an adjacent paddock. Its Northern and Eastern sides abut on the swampy valleys of the streams above mentioned. On the Southern and Western sides it was defended by a rampart and a ditch. The rampart has been much spread by cultivation, and the ditch has been partly obliterated, but the Western side, where it is best preserved, indicates that it was made as a wet moat. The position suggests that this site was used as a seafarers' camp, perhaps by Saxon, Jutish or Danish invaders in the early centuries of our era.

BUCKLER'S HARD is on the Western bank of the Beaulieu river, about two miles distant from Beaulieu down stream. Here John, second Duke of Montagu, the owner of Beaulieu Abbey estate, devised extensive plans for making a town and docks, both for ship-building and for refining sugar, the produce of some West India islands then (about 1740) in his possession. The local abundance of fuel gave promise that sugar might be refined cheaply here, while the Duke, as owner of Beaulieu Abbey, enjoyed immunity from various duties, and possessed the privilege of a free harbour. This scheme, however, came to nought, for the Duke lost his property in the Isle of St. Vincent, apparently the principal source of the sugar, by the Treaty of Aix-la-Chapelle in 1748.

Subsequently Buckler's Hard was taken as a site for shipbuilding by Henry Adams, and from 1753 to 1809 the name of Adams was honourably associated with the shipbuilding yards on Beaulieu river. Forty-three men-of-war were built and launched at Buckler's Hard. The following particulars taken from a paper by G. N. Godwin in The Hampshire Antiquary, Vol. I, tell of bygone days when this shipbuilding industry was a thriving business : "The contract price paid by the Government was £33 10s. a ton, and a seventy-four (guns) was usually at least 18 months upon the stocks. Twenty-seven sail of the line cost over a million and a half to build. A ship of one thousand three hundred tons burden required the felling of more than two thousand average oaks, to supply two thousand loads of timber. One hundred tons of wrought iron, and thirty tons of copper were also needed. When a ship launch was imminent every vehicle and saddle horse within twenty miles was in motion. In default of chairs, many came in tumbrils and waggons. Scaffolds and booths were erected for the spectators, who often numbered ten thousand, and who frequently waited in patience for many hours. But all these things are over. Two brothers, Edward and Walter Adams, finding trade prosperous, undertook to build four men-of-war at one and the same time. The strain upon their resources was too great, failure to deliver the ships in due time caused a fine, and ill-advised litigation was undertaken against the Government with disastrous consequences."

The eventual failure of the shipbuilding industry at Buckler's Hard account for the decrease in the population of Beaulieu. Nowadays, two rows of picturesque red brick and tile roofed cottages, that descend step-wise, on either side of a wide, grass-grown way leading down to a shattered hard on Beaulieu river, are the only relics remaining of the "great days done" at Buckler's Hard. A list of men-of-war built at Buckler's Hard is given on page 98.

BUTTSASH is a place-name that marks a site on Beaulieu Hill-top Heath beside a barrow, and also beside an old road from Applemore, near Dibden, which has claims for consideration as a Roman road to Lepe, or to Stone. cf. the "streets" at Buttsash and Langley in New Forest Perambulations.

DENNY is one of the few old beech woods that can be seen from the Southern Railway in its twisting course through the Forest, and it is the finest in this area. Like Matley its beauty is enhanced by a fringe of self-sown birch trees that surround the irregular verge of this wood, and that make lovely contrast at all times of the year with the background of stately, spreading beech-groves on Denny Hill. Denny Lodge is occupied by the head keeper of the Forest.

EXBURY is a little village situated on the Eastern side of the mouth of the Beaulieu river. There was a chapel of St. Catherine here (pulled down in 1827), which was served by the Cistercians of Beaulieu Abbey.

HATCHET POND is a large, irregular, crescent-shaped sheet of water at the Eastern extremity of Beaulieu Heath. In Richardson King and Driver's map, above mentioned, scattered circles are figured on this site, and marked "Old Marl pits." The site is very exposed and the soil crumbling. Probably this pond, as we now see it, was made by wind-driven water lapping and wasting away the edges of these separate marl pits, till, gradually, they were joined up and became one pond. The name is derived from the hatch gate nearby, separating the heath from the cultivated land. The same name in a similar situation occurs at Hatchet Green, Hale, on the Northern side of Forest. (cf. also Holly Hatch, beneath Sloden; *Hatch*, gate, is a common suffix in the neighbourhood of ancient forests).

LADYCROSS LODGE is situated just within the belt of woodland that bounds the Northern side of Beaulieu Heath. It has been converted into a private residence. During the 1914-18 war much timber (Scots pine planted in 1852) was cut in Frame Heath Enclosure near the railway line.

MATLEY is a beautiful old wood of oak, thorn, and holly, with a fringe of self-sown birch trees growing around its outskirts, and leading down to the dense thickets of alders that mark the line of Matley bog. The fine, matted rootlets of alders, create and increase boggy ground. Walk warily in forest bottoms where alders grow.

PARK HILL is on the site of the "Old Park of Lyndhurst," of which the earliest record dates back to 1291 A.D. In 1300 its acreage and value were thus estimated : "The park of Lyndhurst contains in covert two hundred acres, the pannage thereof is worth yearly when the acorn comes 34s. 3d. Item, the honey in the same park is worth yearly 2s. Item, the herbage can sustain forty beasts and twenty foals and that pasture is worth 23s. 4d.'' The boundary of this old park is still traceable by a wasted bank and ditch. It appears to have been disparked in the 16th century.

An old salt-away from Lymington to Southampton crossed this site. The salterns along the shores of the Solent were worked with profit until the beginning of the 19th century; remains of these salterns can be seen on the Keyhaven marshes near Lymington, and Salter's Hill near St. Leonards is a place-name that records adjacent salterns.

SOWLEY POND in mediaeval times was variously called *Colgrimesmore*, *Frieswater*, or *South legh*. Fish from South legh pond replenished the monastic fish stews at Beaulieu.

In later times iron works were established at Sowley Pond, the blastfurnaces were supplied with fuel from the Forest, and with iron-stone from Hengistbury Head and the Hordle cliffs. "On the Southern shores of the county, particularly the coast of Beauley manor, iron-stone was formerly gathered in some quantity : this, it seems, was generally rolled up by the surf; and such was the eagerness at those times for collecting this mineral, that even in wheat harvest the fields became abandoned, and the shores were thronged with people who gathered and conveyed it to the iron works at Sowley.'' (Vancouver's "General view of Agriculture in Hampshire,'' 1810, at which date the smelting works were still being carried on here). "There will be rain when Sowley hammer is heard,'' is a local proverbial saying that preserves the memory of these iron works.

Owing to its low-lying situation, and to its wooded surroundings, this large sheet of water is hidden, and is nowhere seen as a feature of the local prospect. Tall reeds invade its shallows, fringed landward by birch trees in beautiful contrast with the surrounding Scots pine woods that cast dark reflections in the still water broken here and there by scuttling wild-fowl.

WOODFIDLEY is an old wood of free-grown beeches standing on a knoll to the West of Bishop's Ditch. They rise as landmarks above the tops of the surrounding Scots pine and oaks which were planted 1860-66. The girth of the finest beech, in full prime, on the top of the hill, measures fifteen feet four inches at four feet from the ground; of another, past prime, on the Northern slope of the hill, fifteen feet eight inches. There is a rough track leading from here to Beaulieu Road station.

"Woodfidley rain" is the local name on the Northern side of the Forest for persistent rain from the South-East. Around Woodfidley are favourite hunting grounds for entomologists.

WHITLEY RIDGE LODGE stands on the South-Western edge of the great woods that stretch from Balmer Lawn to Lyndhurst, Denny, Frame wood. It has been converted into a private residence.

CHAPTER SIX

★

Natural Landmarks
Bournemouth and New Forest

ST. CATHERINE'S HILL is capped by a sheet of plateau gravel, lying on Bracklesham Beds. Several hillocks may be seen beside St. Catherine's Hill and Ramsdown, if the sandy track spotted with sandstone be followed by way of Mill Plain to Hurn Station ; along the East base of St. Catherine's Hill these occur as terminals to buttress-like projections from the hill-scarps. The measurements of one may be taken as typical. It rises on the East side twenty-eight feet six inches in forty-eight paces up ; about the same on the North and South sides ; on the West side it rises, from a spur ridge that projects and descends from the hill-scarp, seven feet in fifteen paces up ; the top is about four paces across, with peaty sandfloor.

BLACKWATER FIRS stand on the West base of St. Catherine's Hill ; here, beside the road from Christchurch to Hurn, rises an isolated conical hillock, marked *Tumulus* in the six-inch O.S. sheet. It is covered by rhododendron undergrowth, above which fine Scots and Austrian pines form an overhead canopy. There is no ditch around the base of this hillock. It rises thirty-seven feet in forty-six paces up ; the top is three paces

Sloden Hill —from Splash bridge.

H.S

83

across East to West, from North to South it slopes gently upward for three paces and downward for eight paces, the floor is sandy, covered with pine roots and needles. I think that this hillock is of natural formation.

On the East side of the railway from Christchurch to Ringwood, threequarters of a mile South of Avon Castle, there lies beside WATTON FORD a stretch of heathland on Bracklesham Beds whereon rises a curious group of cushion-topped mounds, some large, some small, some scatterd, some aligned in switch-back rise and fall; they are surrounded by boggy soil, rabbits work freely in these mounds and their scrapes reveal pure, whitish sand as the subsoil. This group shows good examples of sand landmarks naturally formed by denudation beneath the elements.

MOUNT ARARAT AND GREEN MOUNT. Boveridge Heath (near Verwood) whereon rises Mount Ararat, has recently been enclosed, and planted with conifers by the Forestry Commission. In order to prepare this waste for planting, furze and heath have been burnt, and drain ditches dug down Wild Church Bottom—with result that Mount Ararat is now of comparatively easy access on foot. The soil is Bagshot Beds, sand, clay, and gravel, and the Mount stands about two hundred and fifty feet above the sea, surrounded by hummocks and hollows on the North, East, and South sides, from which its final rise is about thirty-five feet in fifty paces up, while on the West side it falls continuously and abruptly for about seventy feet to Wild Church Bottom. Its top is a bare flat of sandy clay ten paces across in rough circle, strewn with sandstone— lumps of which outcrop on the summit footpaths, and four old Austrian pines crown this landmark that stands for Dorset, near the Hants and Dorset boundary.

The West hill-side of Mount Ararat should be descended to the boggy level of Wild Church Bottom, where, looking South, a most arresting view may be obtained of GREEN MOUNT. From here it appears as an abrupt cone—but further survey shows that Green Mount is the terminal of a ridge rising from South to North. It rises on the East, North, and West sides about fifty-two feet in seventy paces up. The top is now (after burning) clearly seen, dinted with numerous hollows, apparently diggings for sandstone. Exploratory digging, two feet down, in one of these hollows, yielded undisturbed sandy soil and sandstone. The Green Mount name is local, suggested by the fern growth on the newly upturned earth of these top hollow diggings, that contrasts with the surrounding heath-clad hills.

KING BARROW, near Cripplestile, is a landmark visible from afar, and stands about three hundred feet above the sea, one hundred and fifty paces South of the Fordingbridge-Cranborne road. *King*, may denote pre-eminence—which it has, *Barrow*, supposed resemblance to a burial mound—which it has not. The soil is Bagshot Beds, and the mount rises on the North-East side, thirty-three feet in eighty paces up, and on the South-West side, fifty-one feet in one hundred and one paces up. It is surrounded by hummocks and hollows and moorland growth. The top is flat, grass-grown, undisturbed by diggings, excepting a central post-hole which probably marks bonfire rejoicings, and measures seventeen paces from North-East to South-West, and ten paces from North-West to South-East. The paths up the mount reveal the subsoil, sand, gravel, and sandy clay, washed and pitted by rainwater runnels. Below King Barrow, amid heathland towards the South, there rises a lesser mound of similar natural formation.

BLACK BARROW stands on forest moorland bordering the South-Eastern side of Dockens Water. The soil is Bracklesham Beds. This hillock is oval in shape, with long axis from East to West, and it is the Eastern terminal of a sandy ridge that gradually rises from the West; its vegetation differs from that of its peaty surroundings, if such growth dividing-line be taken as the base of the hillock, it rises about twenty-eight feet in seventy paces up. The top is pitted by random diggings, the purpose of which is not apparent. Rabbit burrows abound showing the subsoil to be white sand. All the surface indications on and around this hillock signify that it has been denuded by natural, elemental agency.

FIR POUND, Ogden's Purlieu, stands beside a bog bordering the North-Western side of Dockens Water, about two hundred yards from Black Barrow, and is on similar soil. Prior to 1789 an oval enclosure was made here that measures four hundred and sixty paces around, and is bounded by an outside ditch and an inside bank. Fir Pound hillock stands on the North-West boundary of this enclosure. It rises about eighteen feet in forty paces up, the top has no sign of diggings, and measures five paces across. Rabbit burrows show the subsoil to be white sand and pebble stones. Old, wizened Scots pine are scattered all over Fir Pound. This oval enclosure is shown in the 1789 survey map of the New Forest, tree-planted. Scots pine were first planted in the New Forest at Ocknell clump in 1775, which suggests that the wizened pines in Fir Pound may date back to about that period. I do not think that the hand of man has been concerned in the formation of this hillock.

A nameless mount is OGDEN'S PURLIEU domi-nates and terminates an isolated ridge on the North-West of Fir Pound bog. The soil is Bracklesham Beds. On the East and West side it rises forty-four feet in one hundred and eight paces up, on the South side its slope is long and gradual, on the North side it rises eleven feet in twenty-one paces up, and the base level of such rise continues Northward as a ridge, pitted and littered with diggings for sandstone for about two hundred paces, then falling towards the North. The top of the mount is six paces across, and scattered sandstone lie on the surface, bearing witness to sandstone capping that fortifies this ridge. Rabbit scrapes on the mount sides reveal white sand.

SLODEN HILL. On the South-East margin of Old Sloden Wood an eminent hillock stands on the moorland that slopes down to Dockens Water. The soil is Bracklesham Beds. It rises on the East and West sides about fifty-six feet in one hundred and one paces up, on the North side thirty-six feet in forty-eight paces up, on the South side its slope is long and gradual. The top is much riddled by hole diggings and hummocks of upturn, caused by rabbit extermination ; measurement is thereby prevented. The said upturn shows white sand mingled with sandstone as the subsoil. Following the hillside towards the East, there rises another, but lower, hillock, which, like the above, is connected with Sloden Hill by a rise. Both compare in position with the hillocks that project from the East side of St. Catherine's Hill (*supra*).

BROWN LOAF, Crane's Moor, Burley, stands on the North side of the railway from Ringwood to Brockenhurst. The soil is Bagshot Beds. Approached from the North "Brown Loaf" appears to be a conical hillock, and rises thirty-nine feet in sixty-five paces up ; when the top is reached, it will be found that this hillock, like Green Mount and Black Barrow (*supra*), is the terminal of a ridge, about twenty paces in length from North to South, then falling eighteen feet in thirty paces to the edge of the railway cutting, the North scarp of which is covered here with slabs and nodules of brown sandstone, testifying the sandstone capping that fortifies this ridge. The prefix *Brown* may apply to contrast in colour of material found in this hillock, and the adjacent white sand-pits, and the suffix *Loaf*, to the sugar-loaf profile of this hillock as seen on the North side.

PEAL HILL rises on moorland, East of the Southern Railway, and about half a mile from Decoy Pond Farm. The soil is Barton sand. This hill is included in my list only as an example of false attribution to a natural eminence—that it was the site of a *Peel* (North country = small castle), *cf. Partinopex de Blois*, by William Stewart Rose, 1807, note p. 203, a wholly misleading attribution. On the North, South, and West sides it rises about thirty-six feet in ninety paces up, on the East side twenty-five feet in sixty paces up. Its top is flat and oval, one hundred and four paces North to South, fifty paces East to West. The subsoil of the top is sandy peat and gravel. This hill is natural, and is a large example of an isolated eminence produced by denudation beneath the elements.

BARNEY BARNS HILL stands in Dibden Bottom, one hundred and fifty paces South of the road from Hythe to Beaulieu Road Station. The soil is Barton sand, and the hill rises from boggy moorland, gradually, with long axis from East to West, but more abruptly on the North and South sides which measure about thirty feet in seventy paces up. The top is entirely overgrown, and the humps and hollows that cover the floor are thereby concealed. The subsoil appears to be peaty sand. The base of this hill may approximately be regarded as an oval of three hundred and ninety paces. J. R. Wise in *The New Forest*, p. 197, refers to Barney Barns Hill as "apparently of sepulchral character." I do not agree with his estimate, but consider that it is a denuded sand hillock.

CHAPTER SEVEN

★

A List of Forest Terms

The Norman origin of the New Forest is attested by the French terms explained below, many of which still survive. F. = French. A.S. = Anglo-Saxon.

FOREST

F. *Forêt*. A tract of wild country privileged for beasts and fowls of Forest, Chase and Warren, constituted, bounded and possessed by the King only as his hunting ground, having Forest courts, officers, and special laws of its own, whereas a chase, a park, or a warren were the hunting grounds of the subject, after grant from the King, and offenders were liable to the common law.

VERT

F. *Vert*, green. "Every tree that doth grow within the Forest, as well that which is called Hault Boys (F. *hautbois*), as that which is called South Boys (F. wood's *Forest Laws*.)

The principal "Hault Boys" of the Forest are now Oak, Beech, Sweet Chestnut, Birch, Yew, Alder, Whitebeam, Ash (rare), Scots Pine, Larch, Spruce Fir, and "fancy trees," as they are called locally, i.e., Douglas and Silver Fir, and other varieties.

The principal "South Boys" are now Holly, Thorn, Crab-apple, Sallow, Furze, and Sweet-Gale (or Bog-

Myrtle). Spindle and Dogwood may be found exceptionally around Sloden, and stray Junipers are remembered by old woodmen, but have died out.

"Ragged Boys hill," near Sloden, preserves this Norman-French word *Bois*, boys, *Ragged*, rough. (cf. *Ragged* Appleshaw, near Andover).

VENISON

F. *Venaison*. Flesh of beasts of Forest or Chase. (See page 96.)

COURTS AND OFFICERS OF THE FOREST

JUSTICE SEAT. Court of the Chief Justice in Eyre.

F. *Eire*, journey, way. This was the principal Court of the Forest, and was held before the Justice in Eyre, or chief itinerant Judge. The last Justice Seat in Eyre was held at Lyndhurst, 1669-70.

WOODMOTE OR COURT OF ATTACHMENT

A.S. *Mot*, a meeting. F. *Attacher*, to attach. This was a "Court of inquest at which, if the offence charged seemed capable of being proved the offender could be committed for trial at the next Swainmote. In place of being held every forty days as ordered by law, it was wont to be held at the will of the chief officers of the Forest." *Victoria History of Hampshire*, Vol. II Forestry and the New Forest.

COURT OF SWAINMOTE

A.S. *Swain*, freeholder of the Forest. This was a Court where offenders were tried, and if convicted, remanded for judgment at the next Justice Seat, and matters connected with the management of the Forest were considered. The Verderers were supposed to hold three Swainmotes in each year and freeholders had to attend to serve on juries. This Court still continues to be held subject to certain changes made by the New Forest Act, 1877.

LORD WARDEN

F. *Gardien*, a guardian. The chief officer of the Forest,

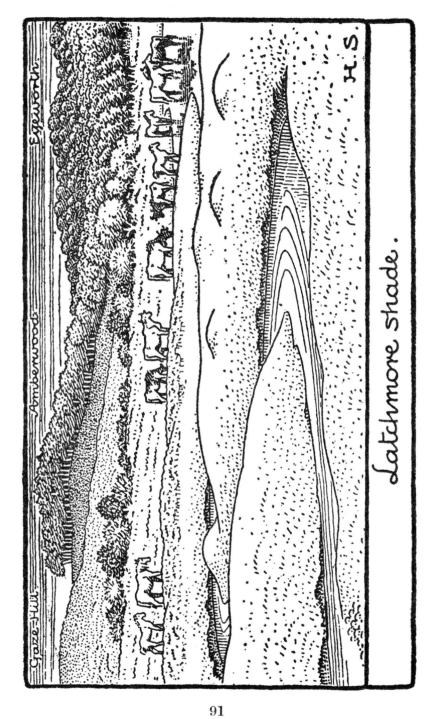

Latchmore shade.

Gaze-Hill   Amberwood   Epworth   H. S.

after the Justice in Eyre, appointed by the King. This office fell into abeyance in 1850.

VERDERER

F. *Vert*, green. Previous to the Act of 1877 there were four Verderers chosen by the King and elected by the freeholders, to adjudicate specially on offences relating to Vert and Venison in the Swainmote Court. An axe was their symbol of office. By the New Forest Act, 1877, six Verderers are now elected by (1) Parliamentry voters of any parish of which a part is within the perambulation of the Forest, (2) those who are on the register of persons entitled to rights of common; with an official Verderer appointed by the Crown, who presides. Verderers have all power and jurisdiction in the Forest as if they were justices of the peace.

REGARDER

F. *Regarder*, to view. There were twelve Regarders appointed by the King, or the Justice in Eyre. Their duties were to survey and view Vert and Venison, to enquire into offences, and to make presentments thereto.

RANGER

F. *Ranger*, to range. He was appointed by the Lord Warden, and was solely concerned with the Purlieus of the Forest. If deer strayed out of the Forest into a Purlieu, his duty was to chase them back into the Forest.

AGISTOR

F. *Gesir*, to lie, from Latin *jacere*, to lie. There were four Agistors appointed by the King. Their duties were connected with agisments, i.e., payments made in respect of cattle, etc., levant (afoot) and couchant (lying) in the Forest, and due to the King.

Since the New Forest Act of 1877 the Agistors are servants of the Verderers.

FORESTERS OR KEEPERS

Their duty was, and is, to watch over both Vert and Venison, and to apprehend anyone who violates Forest laws and regulations within their Walks. A horn was their symbol of office. They are now appointed by the Deputy Surveyor.

WOODWARDS NOW CALLED WOODMEN

Their duty was, and is, connected with the Vert. A bill-hook was their symbol of office. They are subordinate to the keepers and are appointed by the Deputy Surveyor.

HAYWARD

F. *Haie*, hedge, and *gardein*, a guardian. He was, and is, an officer belonging to the out-bounds of the Forest, whose duty is to see that the boundary fences of the commons adjacent to the Forest are kept up, and to pound cattle, etc., that have strayed. He is now appointed by the Parish Council or Meeting. Mr. Arthur Arnold, of Wickham, tells me that in the Forest of Bere (around Bishop's Waltham) this officer is called "*Howard*"—Query. *Hogward*, i.e., the guardian of pannage payments.

RIGHTS OF COMMON AND OF FUEL IN THE FOREST

PASTURE

F. *Pasture*. "All manner of beasts are commonable within a forest, except geese, goats, sheep and swine. . . . Pannage is taken for the Agistment of any kind of mast of trees to feed the said swine or hogs withall." Manwood.

ESTOVER

F. *Estover, Estovoir*, necessaries. The right attached to certain houses of having fuel from the old woods in the Forest. Now called "sign-wood," i.e., assigned wood, the owners of this right being informed where they will find the wood that has been assigned to them, and then they may cart it away. Such wood is cut up and measured by the cord, that is, eight feet long, four feet high, and four feet wide, or equivalent measurements.

TURBARY

F. *Torberie*, turf, sod. The right of digging turf in a specified part of the Forest. Under favourable conditions, a good turf cutter will cut one thousand turves in a day.

OFFENCES IN THE FOREST

ASSART

F. *Assortir*, to make plain, i.e., to root up woods and to break up for *tillage* the ground on which they stood.

PURPRESTURE

F. *Pourpris*, encroachment upon another. Any *encroachment* "be it in building, enclosure, or by using any liberty or privilege without lawful warrant to do so."—Manwood.

WASTE

F. *Wast*, *faire Wast*, to lay waste, e.g., Cutting down a tree, distinguished from *Assart* by the ground not being broken up for tillage on which the tree stood.

MISCELLANEOUS

PURLIEU

F. *Pur*, exempt, *Lieu*, place. Land on the confines of the Forest that has been wrongfully afforested in past times, and subsequently disafforested.

PAWNAGE OR PANNAGE

F. *Pasnage*, "monie for feeding swine with mast." A term used either for beech and oak mast, or for the money paid for such feed.

LAWN

F. *Lande*, a wild grassy plain, e.g., Balmer Lawn,

94

Butt's Lawn, Park Hill Lawn, Mill Lawn, etc.

CHIMINAGE

F. *Chemin*, road. This was a toll paid for passage through the Forest with carriage of anything by cart or on horseback.

EXPEDITATION

Latin, *ex*, from, *pede*, a foot. Dogs capable of chasing deer, and belonging to owners living within the Forest, were by law liable to have "three claws of the forefoot cut off by the skin," or pay a fine. "Henry the Second was the first that began to cut off the claws of the fore-feet of the Mastives : and therefore he called that manner of torment Expeditatio Mastivorum. . . . Ex pede, of the hurt or maim they have of the foot." Manwood. Expeditation, or "lawing," was not the cruel hardship in practise that it may appear to have been in precept. In practise it was a threat that such mutilation would be exacted if a fee of 1s. a year was not paid. That such fees were frequently paid and recorded, is clearly shown in *Thirty-five Years in the New Forest* by the Hon. Gerald Lascelles. P. 78, et seq.

CHAPTER EIGHT

★

Notes on the Forest

In *Select Pleas of the Forest*, edited for the Selden
Society by G. J. Turner, Manwood's list of "Beasts of
the Forest" is thus revived—

"Manwood in his 'Treatise on the Forest Laws,'
which was written at the end of the sixteenth century,
declared that were there five beasts of the forest, the
hart, the hind, the wild boar, and the wolf, the hare, the
hart and the hind being respectively the male and female
of the red deer. But although Manwood did not include
the fallow deer in the class of beasts of the forest, he
inserted it in another class with the fox, the marten and
the roe, which he called beasts of the chase. The law,
however, recognised no such distinction between the red
deer and the fallow deer; for if the words 'beasts of the
forest' have any legal significance, they must refer to
those beasts which are the particular subject of the
forest laws, and as the laws relating to the red deer
were precisely the same as those relating to the fallow
deer, both species ought to be placed in the same class.

"Again, Manwood's exclusion of the roe from the
beasts of the forest, although true in his own time, was
not true of the period under our consideration. During
the thirteenth century the roe was the subject of the
forest laws in all parts of England. . . .

96

"The hare should have no place in his list of beasts of the forest. If we look through the rolls of the forests, we find that except in a few special instances, the hare was not preserved by the forest laws. . . . Again, Manwood's inclusion of the wolf in the class of beasts of the forest was entirely unwarranted. . . . The wolf so far from being in any way preserved, was treated as a noxious beast which ought to be exterminated.

"Thus it may be confidently asserted that there were in general four beasts of the forest, and four only, the red deer, the fallow deer, the roe and the wild boar, the only exception being that in a few districts the hare was also made subject to the forest laws."

As to wild boars, the following reference is of interest, from a letter by Mr. J. E. Harting, Times Literary Supplement, Oct. 30, 1919 :

"Charles I imported some (wild boars) from France and turned them out in the New Forest, where, according to Aubrey, they much increased and became terrible to travellers. However, in the civill warres," he says, 'they were destroyed.' This was written in 1689."

PERAMBULATIONS OF THE NEW FOREST

The first Perambulation recorded was made in 1289 (8th year of Edward I). The next in 1301 (29th year of Edward I). The last in 1681 (22nd year of Charles II). Translations of all three Perambulations may be found in *Topographical Remarks upon the New Forest*, by Percival Lewis, p. 173 et seq. cf. also *A Map showing the Ancient and Modern Areas of the New Forest*, by W. J. C. Moens, 1903.

WALKS OF THE NEW FOREST AND
ACREAGE THEREOF

The New Forest is divided into 15 Walks, as follows :

97

Burley, Holmsley, Bolderwood, Eyeworth, Ashley, Broomy, Rhinefield, Wilverley, Whitley Ridge, Lady Cross, Denny, Ashurst, Ironshill, Castle Malwood, Bramble Hill.

Total area of the New Forest District : 92,395 acres, of which

62,648 Acres are Forest.
27,658   ,,   ,, Private Property.
2,089   ,,   ,, Freehold and Copyhold of the Crown

POPULATION

Showing the changes in population of the principal towns and villages in the New Forest District over a period of one hundred and eleven years.

	1810	1911	1921	
Beaulieu	1384	986	1000	
Boldre	1743	2504	2394	
Bramshaw	303	510	470	Bramshaw E
Brockenhurst	632	2048	2159	270
Burley	241	1208	1333	
Fordingbridge	2335	3456	3393	
Lymington	2388	4329	4598	
Lyndhurst	882	2406	2560	
Minstead	764	892	800	
Ringwood	3214	5055	5128	

A LIST OF MEN-OF-WAR BUILT AT BUCKLER'S HARD

Compiled by R. B. Adams. (The Hampshire Antiquary, Vol. II)

1745 *Surprize*, 24 guns "Bewley, Wyatt & Co."
1746 *Scorpion*, 14 guns "Bewley."
1749 *Woolwich*, 44 guns,   ,,
1749 *Fowey*, 24 guns "Beaulieu."
1749 *Mermaid*, 24 guns   ,,

1753	*Lion*, transport, 151 tons, 4 guns	"Beaulieu, H. Adams."
1756	*Gibraltar*, 20 guns	,, ,,
1757	*Coventry*, 28 guns	,, ,,
1758	*Levant*, 28 guns	,, ,,
1758	*Thames*, 32 guns	,, ,,
1760	*Heyling*, hoy, 132 tons, 4 guns	,, ,,
1746	*Europa*, 64 guns (Leap)	,, ,,
1772	*Hannibal*, 50 guns	"Bucklershard."
1773	*Thetis*, 32 guns	,,
1773	*Greyhound*, 28 guns	,,
1773	*Triton*, 28 guns	,,
1773	*Vigilant*, 64 guns	,, "Adams & Co."
1774	*Sybil*, 28 guns	,, ,,
1777	*Romulus*, 44 guns	,, "H. Adams."
1779	*Brilliant*, 28 guns	,, ,,
1779	*Sybil*, afterwards *Garland*, 28 guns	,, ,,
1781	*Agamemnon*, 64 guns	,, "Adams."
1782	*Gladiator*, 44 guns	,, "H. Adams."
1783	*Heroine*, 32 guns	,,
1783	*Indefatigable*, 64 guns (reduced to 44 guns 1794)	,, ,,
1785	*Illustrious*, 74 guns	"Bucklershard, Adams."
1787	*Sheerness*, 44 guns	,, "H. Adams."
1790	*Beaulieu*, 40 guns	,, ,,
1793	*Santa Margaritta*, 56 guns	,, ,,
1793	*Penelope*, 36 guns	,, ,,
1794	*Cerberus*, 32 guns	,, "Adams."
1796	*Bittern*, 16 guns	,, ,,
1797	*Snake*, 14 guns	,, ,,
1797	*Boadicea*, 38 guns	,, ,,
1800	*Spencer*, 74 guns	,, ,,
1801	*L'Aigle*, 36 guns	,, ,,

1801	*Snipe*, 14 carronades	,,	,,
1803	*Euryalus*, 36 guns	,,	,,
1804	*Swiftsure*, 74 guns "B. Adams's yard, Buckler's Hard."
1806-7	*Columbine*, 18 guns "Bucklershard"
1807 (?)	*Hussar*, 36 guns	,,	(Laid down in 1804.)
1808	*Victorious*, 74 guns	,,
1809 (?)	*Hannibal*, 74 guns "Adams's yard, Bucklershard."

RAINFALL

The annual rainfall in the District may be inferred from the following figures, taken on an average of records for 10 years, 1909-1919.

Lyndhurst ... ... 39.31 inches
Cuckoo Hill, South Gorley, Fordingbridge 35.90 ,,
Lymington ... ... 33.37 ,,

Fritham and Cadnam records do not cover the period. Such as they supply approximate to the rainfall of Lyndhurst, while Dockens, Linwood (also incomplete), approximates to Cuckoo Hill. Both latter places are on the verge of open heathlands, while Lyndhurst, Fritham and Cadnam are surrounded by woodlands. The local rainfall on the seaboard appears to be less than that inland nearby. A Purbeck resident gave me this formula, "Our hills scratch the clouds and they cry inland." A formula which serves along our seaboard.

Mr. Sidney B. Rake, of Oaklands, Fordingbridge, has the longest unbroken record of local rainfall in this district, dating back to 1874, giving an average rainfall from 1875 to 1921 of 31.83 inches, and for 10 years, 1909-1919, of 36.10 inches.

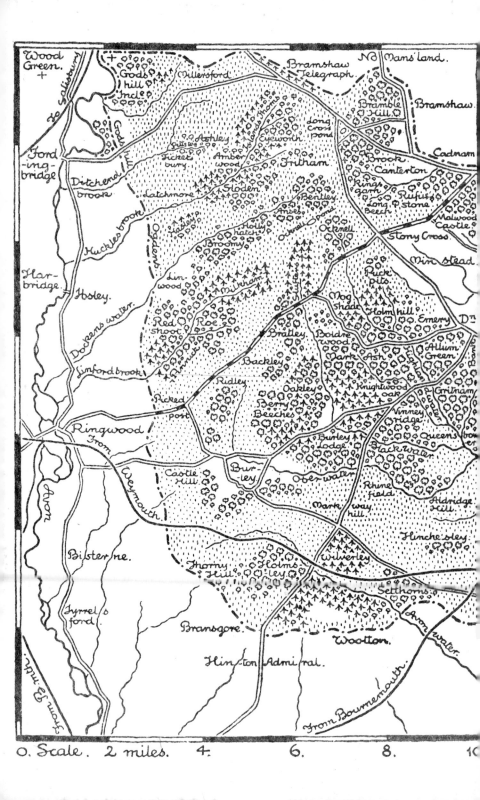

Wood Green.

Bramshaw Telegraph.   No Mans' land.

to Salisbury

Gods hill   Millersford   Bramble Hill   Bramshaw

Fording-bridge   Ditchend brook   Ashley   Eyeworth   Brook   Cadnam

Latchmore   Sloden   Fritham   Canterton

Huckles brook   Amber wood   Kings garn   Rufus stone

Harbridge   Bentley   Long Beech   Malwood Castle

Ibsley.   Holly hatch   Ocknell   Stony Cross.

Broomy   Ocknell pond   Minstead.

Dockens water.   Linwood   Milkham   Puck pits.

Linford brook.   Red shoot   Roe   Mog Shade   Holm hill   Emery   Dn

Bratley   Boldre wood   Holm hill

Picked post   Ridley   Backley   Mark Ash   Allum Green

Ringwood   Oakley   Knightwood oak   Gritnam

From   Berry Beeches   Vinney ridge   Queens bower

Weymouth   Burley Lodge   Black water

Castle Hill.   Bur-ley   Ober water   Rhine field   Aldridge hill

Avon   Mark way hill   Hinchesley.

Bisterne.   Thorny Hill   Holmsley   Wilverley   Setthorns

Tyrrel's ford.   Bransgore.   Wootton.   Avon water

Hinton Admiral.   From Bournemouth

from B. mth

O. Scale. 2 miles. 4. 6. 8. 10